A MINSTREL IN
FRANCE

1500 BOOKS

New York, NY

Copyright © 2006 by 1500 Books, LLC

All rights reserved. No part of this book may be used or reproduced in any manner whatsoever without written permission from the publisher except in the case of brief quotations for reviews or articles. For information contact 1500 Books, www.1500books.net.

Designed by Jillian Harris
Art Direction by Bruce Hall

Printed in Canada

A MINSTREL IN FRANCE

HARRY LAUDER

1500 BOOKS

New York, NY

CHAPTER I

Yon days! Yon palmy, peaceful days! I go back to them, and they are as a dream. I go back to them again and again, and live them over. Yon days of another age, the age of peace, when no man dared even to dream of such times as have come upon us.

It was in November of 1913, and I was setting forth upon a great journey, that was to take me to the other side of the world before I came back again to my wee hoose amang the heather at Dunoon. My wife was going with me, and my brother-in-law, Tom Vallance, for they go everywhere with me. But my son John was coming with us only to Glasgow, and then, when we set out for Liverpool and the steamer that was to bring us to America he was to go back to Cambridge. He was near done there, the bonnie laddie. He had taken his degree as Bachelor of Arts, and was to set out soon upon a trip around the world.

Was that no a fine plan I had made for my son? That great voyage he was to have, to see the world and all its peoples! It was proud I was that I could give it to him. He was – but it may be I'll tell you more of John later in this book!

My pen runs awa' with me, and my tongue, too, when I think of my boy John.

We came to the pier at Dunoon, and there she lay, the little ferry steamer, the black smoke curling from her stack straight up to God. Ah, the braw day it was! There was a frosty sheen upon the heather, and the Clyde was calm as glass. The tops of the hills were coated with snow, and they stood out against the horizon like great big sugar loaves.

We were a' happy that day! There was a crowd to see us off. They had come to bid me farewell and godspeed, all my friends and my relations, and I went among them, shaking them by the hand and thinking of the long whiles before I'd be seeing them again. And then all my goodbyes were said, and we went aboard, and my voyage had begun.

I looked back at the hills and the heather, and I thought of all I was to do and see before I saw those hills again. I was going half way round the world and back again. I was going to wonderful places to see wonderful things and curious faces. But oftenest the thought came to me, as I looked at my son, that him I would see again before I saw the heather and the hills and all the friends and the relations I was leaving behind me. For on his trip around the world he was to meet us in Australia! It was easier to leave him, easier to set out, knowing that, thinking of that!

Wonderful places I went to, surely. And wonderful things I saw and heard. But the most wonderful thing of all that I was to see or hear upon that voyage I did not dream of nor foresee. How was a mortal man to foresee? How was he to dream of it?

Could I guess that the very next time I set out from Dunoon pier the peaceful Clyde would be dotted with patrol boats, dashing hither and thither! Could I guess that everywhere there would be boys in khaki, and women weeping, and that my boy, John! Ah, but I'll not tell you of that now.

Peaceful the Clyde had been, and peaceful was the Mersey when we sailed from Liverpool for New York. I look back on yon voyage – the last I took that way in days of peace. Next time! Destroyers to guard us from the Hun and his submarines, and to lay us a safe course through the mines. And sailor boys, about their guns, watching, sweeping the sea every minute for the flash of a sneaking pirate's periscope showing for a second above a wave!

But then! It was a quiet trip, with none but the ups and doons of every Atlantic crossing – more ups than doons, I'm telling you!

I was glad to be in America again, glad to see once more the friends I'd made. They turned out to meet me and to greet me in New York, and as I travelled across the continent to San Francisco it was the same. Everywhere I had friends; everywhere they came crowding to shake me by the hand with a "How are you the day, Harry?"

It was a long trip, but it was a happy one. How long ago it seems now, as I write, in this new day of war! How far away are all the common, kindly things that then I did not notice, and that now I would give the world and a' to have back again!

Then, everywhere I went, they pressed their dainties upon me whenever I sat down for a sup and a bite. The board groaned with plenty. I was in a rich country, a country where there was enough for all, and to spare. And now, as I am writing I am travelling again across America. And there is not enough. When I sit down at table there is a card of Herbert Hoover's, bidding me be careful how I eat and what I choose. Ay, but he has no need to warn me! Well I know the truth, and how America is helping to feed her allies over there, and so must be sparing herself.

To think of it! In yon far day the world was all at peace. And now that great America, that gave so little thought to armies and to cannon, is fighting with my ain British against the Hun!

It was in March of 1914 that we sailed from San Francisco, on the tenth of the month. It was a glorious day as we stood on the deck of the old Pacific liner *Sonoma*. I was eager and glad to be off. To be sure, America had been kinder to me than ever, and I was loath, in a way, to be leaving her and all the friends of mine she held – old friends of years, and new ones made on that trip. But I was coming back. And then there was one great reason for my eagerness that few folk knew – that my son John was coming to meet me in Australia. I was missing him sore already.

They came aboard the old tubby liner to see us off, friends by the score. They kept me busy shaking hands.

"Good-by, Harry," they said. And "Good luck, Harry," they cried. And just before the bugles sounded all ashore I heard a few of them crooning an old Scots song:

"Will ye no come back again?"

"Aye, I'll come back again!" I told them when I heard them.

"Good, Harry, good!" they cried back to me. "It's a promise! We'll be waiting for you – waiting to welcome you!"

And so we sailed from San Francisco and from America, out through the Golden Gate, toward the sunset. Here was beauty for me, who loved it new beauty, such as I had not seen before. They were quiet days, happy days, peaceful days. I was tired after my long tour, and the days at sea rested me, with good talk when I craved it, and time to sleep, and no need to give thought to trains, or to think, when I went to bed, that in the night they'd rouse me from my sleep by switching my car and giving me a bump.

We came first to Hawaii, and I fell in love with the harbor of Honolulu as we sailed in. Here, at last, I began to see the strange sights and hear the strange sounds I had been looking forward to ever since I left my wee hoose at Dunoon. Here was something that was different from anything that I had ever seen before.

We did not stay so long. On the way home I was to stay over and give a performance in Honolulu, but not now. Our time was given up to sight seeing, and to meeting some of the folk of the islands. They ken hospitality! We made many new friends there, short as the time was. And, man! The lassies! You want to cuddle the first lassie you meet when you step ashore at Honolulu. But you don't – if the wife is there!

It was only because I knew that we were to stop longer on the way back that I was willing to leave Honolulu at all. So we sailed on, toward Australia. And now I knew that my boy was about setting out on his great voyage around the world. Day by day I would get out the map, and try to prick the spot where he'd be.

And I'd think: "Aye! When I'm here John'll be there! Will he be nearer to me than now?"

Thinking of the braw laddie, setting out, so proud and happy, made me think of my ain young days. My father couldna' give me such a chance as my boy was to have. I'd worked in the mines before I was John's age. There'd been no Cambridge for me – no trip around the world as a part of my education. And I thanked God that he was letting me do so much for my boy.

Aye, and he deserved it, did John! He'd done well at Cambridge; he had taken honors there. And soon he was to go up to London to read for the Bar. He was to be a barrister, in wig and gown, my son, John!

It was of him, and of the meeting we were all to have in Australia, that I thought, more than anything else, in the long, long days upon the sea. We sailed on from Honolulu until we came to Paga-Paga. So it is spelled, but all the natives call it Panga-Panga.

Here I saw more and yet more of the strange and wonderful things I had thought upon so long back, in Dunoon. Here I saw mankind, for the first time, in a natural state. I saw men who wore only the figleaf of old Father Adam, and a people who lived from day to day, and whom the kindly earth sustained.

They lived entirely from vegetables and from clear crystal streams and upon marvelous fish from the sea. Ah, how I longed to stay in Paga-Paga and be a natural man. But I must go on. Work called me back to civilization and sorrowfully I heeded its call and waved good-by to the natural folk of Paga-Paga!

It was before I came to Paga-Paga that I wrote a little verse inspired by Honolulu. Perhaps, if I had gone first to Paga-Paga – don't forget to put in the n and call it Panga-Panga when you say it to yourself! – I might have written it of that happy island of the natural folk. But I did not, so here is the verse:

> I love you, Honolulu, Honolulu I love you!
> You are the Queen of the Sea!
> Your valleys and mountains
> Your palais and fountains
> Forever and ever will be dear to me!

I wedded a simple melody to those simple, heartfelt lines, and since then I have sung the song in pretty nearly every part of the world – and in Honolulu itself.

Our journey was drawing to its end. We were coming to a strange land indeed. And yet I knew there were Scots folk there – where in the world are there not? I thought they would be glad to see me, but how could I be sure? It was a far, far cry from Dunoon and the Clyde and the frost upon the heather on the day I had set out.

We were to land at Sydney. I was a wee bit impatient after we had made our landfall, while the old *Sonoma* poked her way along. But she would not be hurried by my impatience. And at last we came to the Sydney Heads – the famous Harbor Heads. If you have never seen it I do not know how better to tell you of it than to say that it makes me think of the entrance to a great cave that has no roof. In we went – and were within that great, nearly landlocked harbor.

And what goings on there were! The harbor was full of craft, both great and sma'. And each had all her bunting flying. Oh, they were braw in the sunlight, with the gay colors and the bits of flags, all fluttering and waving in the breeze!

And what a din there was, with the shrieking of the whistle and the foghorns and the sirens and the clamor of bells. It took my breath away, and I wondered what was afoot. And on the shore I could see that thousands of people waited, all crowded together by the water side. There were flags flying, too, from all the buildings.

"It must be that the King is coming in on a visit –and I never to have heard of it!" I thought.

And then they made me understand that it was all for me!

If there were tears in my eyes when they made me believe that, will you blame me? There was that great harbor, all alive with the welcome they made for me. And on the shore, they told me, a hundred thousand were waiting to greet me and bid me:

"Welcome, Harry!"

The tramways had stopped running until they had done with their welcome to me. And all over the city, as we drove to our hotel, they roared their welcome, and there were flags along the way.

That was the proudest day I had ever known. But one thing made me wistful and wishful. I wanted my boy to be there with us. I wished he had seen how they had greeted his Dad. Nothing pleased him more than an honor that came to me. And here was an honor indeed – a reception the like of which I had never seen.

CHAPTER II

It was on the twenty-ninth day of March, in that year of 1914 that dawned in peace and happiness and set in blood and death and bitter sorrow, that we landed in Sydney. Soon I went to work. Everywhere my audiences showed me that that great and wonderful reception that had been given to me on the day we landed had been only an earnest of what was to come. They greeted me everywhere with cheers and tears, and everywhere we made new friends, and sometimes found old ones of whom we had not heard for years.

And I was thinking all the time, now, of my boy. He was on his way. He was on the Pacific. He was coming to me, across the ocean, and I could smile as I thought of how this thing and that would strike him, and of the smile that would light up his face now and the look of joy that would come into his eyes at the sudden sighting of some beautiful spot. Oh, aye – those were happy days. When each one brought my boy nearer to me.

One day, I mind, the newspapers were full of the tale of a crime in an odd spot in Europe that none of us had ever heard of before. You mind the place? Serajevo! Aye – we all mind it now! But then we read, and wondered how that outlandish name might be pronounced. A foreigner was murdered – what if he was a prince, the Archduke of Austria? Need we lash ourselves about him?

And so we read, and were sorry, a little, for the puir lady who sat beside the Archduke and was killed with him. And then we forgot it. All Australia did. There was no more in the newspapers. And my son John was coming – coming. Each day he was so many hundred miles nearer to me. And at last he came. We were in Melbourne then, it was near to the end of July.

We had much to talk about – son, and his mother and I. It was long months since we had seen him, and we had seen and done so much. The time flew by. Maybe we did not read the papers so carefully as we might have done. They tell me, they have told me, since then, that in Europe and even in America, there was some warning after Austria moved on Serbia. But I believe that down there in Australia they did not dream of danger; that they were far from understanding the meaning of the news the papers did print. They were so far away!

And then, you ken, it came upon us like a clap of thunder. One night it began. There was war in Europe – real war. Germany had attacked France and Russia. She was moving troops through Belgium. And every Briton knew what that must mean. Would Britain be drawn in? There was the question that was on every man's tongue.

"What do you think, son?" I asked John.

"I think we'll go in," he said. "And if we do, you know, Dad – they'll send for me to come home at once. I'm on leave from the summer training camp now to make this trip."

My boy, two years before, had joined the Territorial army. He was a second lieutenant in a Territorial battalion of the Argyle and Sutherland Highlanders. It was much as if he had been an officer in a National Guard regiment in the United States. The Territorial army was not bound to serve abroad – but who could doubt that it would, and gladly. As it did – to a man, to a man.

But it was a shock to me when John said that. I had not thought that war, even if it came, could come home to us so close – and so soon.

Yet so it was. The next day was the fourth of August – my birthday. And it was that day that Britain declared war upon Germany. We sat at lunch in the hotel at Melbourne when the newsboys began to cry the extras. And we were still at lunch when the hall porter came in from outside.

"Leftenant Lauder!" he called, over and over. John beckoned to him, and he handed my laddie a cablegram.

Just two words there were, that had come singing along the wires half way around the world.

"Mobilize. Return."

John's eyes were bright. They were shining. He was looking at us, but he was not seeing us. Those eyes of his were seeing distant things. My heart was sore within me, but I was proud and happy that it was such a son I had to give my country.

"What do you think, Dad?" he asked me, when I had read the order.

I think I was gruff because I dared not let him see how I felt. His mother was very pale.

"This is no time for thinking, son," I said. "It is the time for action. You know your duty."

He rose from the table, quickly.

"I'm off!" he said.

"Where?" I asked him.

"To the ticket office to see about changing my berth. There's a steamer this week – maybe I can still find room aboard her."

He was not long gone. He and his chum went down together and come back smiling triumphantly.

"It's all right, Dad," he told me. "I go to Adelaide by train and get the steamer there. I'll have time to see you and mother off – your steamer goes two hours before my train."

We were going to New Zealand. And my boy was going home to fight for his country. They would call me too old, I knew – I was forty-four the day Britain declared war.

What a turmoil there was about us! So fast were things moving that there seemed no time for thought, John's mother and I could not realize the full meaning of all that was happening. But we knew that John was snatched away from us just after he had come, and it was hard – it was cruelly hard.

But such thoughts were drowned in the great surging excitement that was all about us. In Melbourne, and I believe it must have been much the same elsewhere in Australia, folks didn't know what they were to do, how they were to take this war that had come so suddenly upon them. And rumors and questions flew in all directions.

Suppose the Germans came to Australia? Was there a chance of that? They had islands, naval bases, not so far away. They were Australia's neighbors. What of the German navy? Was it out? Were there scattered ships, here and there, that might swoop down upon Australia's shores and bring death and destruction with them?

But even before we sailed, next day, I could see that order was coming out of that chaos. Everywhere recruiting offices were opening, and men were flocking to them. No one dreamed, really, of a long war – though John laughed, sadly, when someone said it would be over in four months. But these Australians took no chances; they would offer themselves first, and let it be decided later whether they were needed.

So we sailed away. And when I took John's hand, and kissed him good-by, I saw him for the last time in his civilian clothes.

"Well, son," I said, "you're going home to be a soldier, a fighting soldier. You will soon be commanding men. Remember that you can never ask a man to do something you would no dare to do yourself!"

And, oh, the braw look in the eyes of the bonnie laddie as he tilted his chin up to me!

"I will remember, Dad!" he said.

And so long as a bit of the dock was in sight we could see him waving to us. We were not to see him again until the next January, at Bedford, in England, where he was training the raw men of his company.

Those were the first days of war. The British navy was on guard. From every quarter the whimpering wireless brought news of this German warship and that.

They were scattered far and wide, over the Seven Seas, you ken, when the war broke out. There was no time for them to make a home port. They had their choice, most of them, between being interned in some neutral port and setting out to do as much mischief as they could to British commerce before they were caught. Caught they were sure to be. They must have known it. And some there were to brave the issue and match themselves against England's great naval power.

Perhaps they knew that few ports would long be neutral! Maybe they knew of the abominable war the Hun was to wage. But I think it was not such men as those who chose to take their one chance in a thousand who were sent out, later, in their submarines, to send women and babies to their deaths with their torpedoes!

Be that as it may, we sailed away from Melbourne. But it was in Sydney Harbor that we anchored next – not in Wellington, as we, on the ship, all thought it would be! And the reason was that the navy, getting word that the German cruiser *Emden* was loose and raiding, had ordered our captain to hug the shore, and to put in at Sydney until he was told it was safe to proceed.

We were not much delayed, and came to Wellington safely. New Zealand was all ablaze with the war spirit. There was no hesitation there. The New Zealand troops were mobilizing when we arrived, and every recruiting office was besieged with men. Splendid laddies they were, who looked as if they would give a great account of themselves. As they did – as they did. Their deeds at Gallipoli speak for them and will forever speak for them – the men of Australia and New Zealand.

There the word Anzac was made – made from the first letters of these words: Australian New Zealand Army Corps. It is a word that will never die.

Even in the midst of war they had time to give me a welcome that warmed my heart. And there were pipers with them, too, skirling a tune as I stepped ashore. There were tears in my eyes again, as there had been at Sydney. Every laddie in uniform made me think of my own boy, well off, by now, on his way home to Britain and the duty that had called him.

They were gathering, all over the Empire, those of British blood. They were answering the call old Britain had sent across the seven seas to the far corners of the earth. Even as the Scottish clans gathered of old the greater British clans were gathering now. It was a great thing to see that in the beginning; it has comforted me many a time since, in a black hour, when news was bad and the Hun was thundering at the line that was so thinly held in France.

Here were free peoples, not held, not bound, free to choose their way. Britain could not make their sons come to her aid. If they came they must come freely, joyously, knowing that it was a right cause, a holy cause, a good cause, that called them. I think of the way they came – of the way I saw them rising to the summons, in New Zealand, in Australia, later in Canada. Aye, and I saw more – I saw Americans slipping across the border, putting on Britain's khaki there in Canada, because they knew that it was the fight of humanity, of freedom, that they were entering. And that, too, gave me comfort later in dark times, for it made me know that when the right time came America would take her place beside old Britain and brave France.

New Zealand is a bonnie land. It made me think, sometimes, of the Hielands of Scotland. A bonnie land, and braw are its people. They made me happy there, and they made much of me.

At Christchurch they did a strange thing. They were selling off, at auction, a Union Jack – the flag of Britain. Such a thing had never been done before, or thought of. But here was a reason and a good one. Money was needed for the laddies who were going – needed for all sorts of things. To buy them small comforts, and tobacco, and such things as the government might not be supplying them. And so they asked me to be their auctioneer.

I played a fine trick upon them there in Christchurch. But I was not ashamed of myself, and I think they have forgi'en me – those good bodies at Christchurch!

Here was the way of it. I was auctioneer, you ken – but that was not enough to keep me from bidding myself. And so I worked them up and on – and then I bid in the flag for myself for a hundred pounds – five hundred dollars of American money.

I had my doots about how they'd be taking it to have a stranger carry their flag away. And so I bided a wee. I stayed that night in Christchurch, and was to stay longer. I could wait. Above yon town of Christchurch stretch the Merino Hills. On them graze sheep by the thousand – and it is from those sheep that the true Merino wool comes. And in the gutters of Christchurch there flows, all day long, a stream of water as clear and pure as ever you might hope to see. And it should be so, for it is from artesian wells that it is pumped.

Aweel, I bided that night and by next day they were murmuring in the town, and their murmurs came to me. They thought it wasna richt for a Scotsman to be carrying off their flag – though he'd bought it and paid for it. And so at last they came to me, and wanted to be buying back the flag. And I was agreeable.

"Aye – I'll sell it back to ye!" I told them. "But at a price, ye ken – at a price! Pay me twice what I paid for it and it shall be yours!"

There was a Scots bargain for you! They must have thought me mean and grasping that day. But out they went. They worked for the money. It was but just a month after war had been declared, and money was still scarce and shy of peeping out and showing itself. But, bit by bit, they got the siller. A shilling at a time they raised, by subscription. But they got it all, and brought it to me, smiling the while.

"Here, Harry – here's your money!" they said. "Now give us back our flag!"

Back to them I gave it – and with it the money they had brought, to be added to the fund for the soldier boys. And so that one flag brought three hundred pounds sterling to the soldiers. I wonder did those folk at Christchurch think I would keep the money and make a profit on that flag?

Had it been another time I'd have stayed in New Zealand gladly a long time. It was a friendly place, and it gave us many a new friend. But home was calling me. There was more than the homebound tour that had been planned and laid out for me. I did not know how soon my boy might be going to France. And his mother and I wanted to see him again before he went, and to be as near him as might be.

So I was glad as well as sorry to sail away from New Zealand's friendly shores, to the strains of pipers softly skirling:

"Will ye no come back again?"

We sailed for Sydney on the *Minnehaha*, a fast boat. We were glad of her speed a day or so out, for there was smoke on the horizon that gave some anxious hours to our officers. Some thought the German raider *Emden* was under that smoke. And it would not have been surprising had a raider turned up in our path. For just before we sailed it had been discovered that the man in charge of the principal wireless station in New Zealand was a German, and he had been interned. Had he sent word to German warships of the plans and movements of British ships? No one could prove it, so he was only interned.

Back we went to Sydney. A great change had come since our departure. The war ruled all deed and thought. Australia was bound now to do her part. No less faithfully and splendidly than New Zealand was she engaged upon the enterprise the Hun had thrust upon the world. Everyone was eager for news, but it was woefully scarce. Those were the black, early days, when the German rush upon Paris was being stayed, after the disasters of the first fortnight of the war, at the Marne.

Everywhere, though there was no lack of determination to see the war through to a finish, no matter how remote that might be, the feeling was that this war was too huge, too vast, to last long. Exhaustion would end it. War upon the modern scale could not last. So they said

– in September, 1914! So many of us believed – and this is the spring of the fourth year of the war, and the end is not yet, is not in sight, I fear.

Sydney turned out, almost as magnificently as when I had first landed upon Australian soil, to bid me farewell. And we embarked again upon that same old *Sonoma* that had brought us to Australia. Again I saw Paga-Paga and the natural folk, who had no need to toil nor spin to live upon the fat of the land and be arrayed in the garments that were always up to the minute in style.

Again I saw Honolulu, and, this time, stayed longer, and gave a performance. But, though we were there longer, it was not long enough to make me yield to that temptation to cuddle one of the brown lassies! Aweel, I was not so young as I had been, and Mrs. Lauder – you ken that she was travelling with me?

In the harbor of Honolulu there was a German gunboat, the *Geier*, that had run there for shelter not long since, and had still left a day or two, under the orders from Washington, to decide whether she would let herself be interned or not. And outside, beyond the three mile limit that marked the end of American territorial waters, were two good reasons to make the German think well of being interned. They were two cruisers, squat and ugly and vicious in their gray war paint, that watched the entrance to the harbor as you have seen a cat watching a rat hole.

It was not Britain's white ensign that they flew, those cruisers. It was the red sun flag of Japan, one of Britain's allies against the Hun. They had their vigil in vain, did those two cruisers. It was valor's better part, discretion, that the German captain chose. Aweel, you could no blame him! He and his ship would have been blown out of the water so soon as she poked her nose beyond American waters, had he chosen to go out and fight.

I was glad indeed when we came in sight of the Golden Gate once more, and when we were safe ashore in San Francisco. It had been a nerve-racking voyage in many ways. My wife and I were torn with anxiety about our boy. And there were German raiders loose; one or two had, so far, eluded the cordon the British fleet had flung about the world. One night, soon after we left Honolulu, we were stopped. We thought it was a British cruiser that stopped us, but she would only ask questions – answering those we asked was not for her!

But we were ashore at last. There remained only the trip across the United States to New York and the voyage across the Atlantic home.

CHAPTER III

Now indeed we began to get real news of the war. We heard of how that little British army had flung itself into the maw of the Hun. I came to know something of the glories of the retreat from Mons, and of how French and British had turned together at the Marne and had saved Paris. But, alas, I heard too of how many brave men had died – had been sacrificed, many and many a man of them, to the failure of Britain to prepare.

That was past and done. What had been wrong was being mended now. Better, indeed – ah, a thousand times better! – had Britain given heed to Lord Roberts, when he preached the gospel of readiness and prayed his countrymen to prepare for the war that he in his wisdom had foreseen. But it was easier now to look into the future.

I could see, as all the world was beginning to see, that this war was not like other wars. Lord Kitchener had said that Britain must make ready for a three year war, and I, for one, believed him when others scoffed, and said he was talking so to make the recruits for his armies come faster to the colors. I could see that this war might last for years. And it was then, back in 1914, in the first winter of the war, that I began to warn my friends in America that they might well expect the Hun to drag them into the war before its end. And I made up my mind that I must beg Americans who would listen to me to prepare.

So, all the way across the continent, I spoke, in every town we visited, on that subject of preparedness. I had seen Britain, living in just such a blissful anticipation of eternal peace as America then dreamed of. I had heard, for years, every attempt that was made to induce Britain to increase her army met with the one, unvarying reply.

"We have our fleet!" That was the answer that was made. And, be it remembered, that at sea, Britain – was – prepared! "We have our fleet. We need no army. If there is a Continental war, we may not be drawn in at all. Even if we are, they can't reach us. The fleet is between us and invasion."

"But," said the advocates of preparedness, "we might have to send an expeditionary force. If France were attacked, we should have to help her on land as well as at sea. And we have sent armies to the continent before."

"Yes," the other would reply. "We have an expeditionary force. We can send more than a hundred thousand men across the channel at short notice – the shortest. And we can train more men here, at home, in case of need. The fleet makes that possible."

Aye, the fleet made that possible. The world may well thank God for the British fleet. I do not know, and I do not like to think, what might have come about save for the British fleet. But I do know what came to that expeditionary force that we sent across the channel quickly, to the help of our sore stricken ally, France. How many of that old British army still survive?

They gave themselves utterly. They were the pick and the flower of our trained manhood. They should have trained the millions who were to rise at Kitchener's call. But they could not be held back. They are gone. Others have risen up to take their places – ten for one – a hundred for one! But had they been ready at the start! The bonnie laddies who would be living now, instead of lying in an unmarked grave in France or Flanders! The women whose eyes would never have been reddened by their weeping as they mourned a son or a brother or a husband!

So I was thinking as I set out to talk to my American friends and beg them to prepare – prepare! I did not want to see this country share the experience of Britain. If she needs must be drawn into the war – and so I believed, profoundly, from the time when I first learned the true measure of the Hun – I hoped that she might be ready when she drew her mighty sword.

They thought I was mad, at first, many of those to whom I talked. They were so far away from the war. And already the propaganda of the Germans was at work. Aye, they thought I was raving when I told them I'd stake my word on it. America would never be able to stay out until the end. They listened to me. They were willing to do that. But they listened, doubtingly. I think I convinced few of ought save that I believed myself what I was saying.

I could tell them, do you ken, that I'd thought, at first, as they did! Why, over yon, in Australia, when I'd first heard that the Germans were attacking France, I was sorry, for France is a bonnie land. But the idea that Britain might go in I, even then, had laughed at. And then Britain – had – gone in! My own boy had gone to the war. For all I knew I might be reading of him, any day, when I read of a charge or a fight over there in France! Anything was possible – aye, probable!

I have never called myself a prophet. But then, I think, I had something of a prophet's vision. And all the time I was struggling with my growing belief that this was to be a long war, and a merciless war. I did not want to believe some of the things I knew I must believe. But every day came news that made conviction sink in deeper and yet deeper.

It was not a happy trip, that one across the United States. Our friends did all they could to make it so, but we were consumed by too many anxieties and cares. How different was it from my journey westward – only nine months earlier! The world had changed forever in those nine months.

Everywhere I spoke for preparedness. I addressed the Rotary Clubs, and great audiences turned out to listen to me. I am a Rotarian myself, and I am proud indeed that I may so proclaim myself. It is a great organization. Those who came to hear me were cordial, nearly always. But once or twice I met hostility, veiled but not to be mistaken. And it was easy to trace it to its source. Germans, who loved the country they had left behind them to come to a New World that offered them a better home and a richer life than they could ever have aspired to at home, were often at the bottom of the opposition to what I had to say.

They did not want America to prepare, lest her weight be flung into the scale against Germany. And there were those who hated Britain. Some of these remembered old wars and grudges that sensible folk had forgotten long since; others, it may be, had other motives. But there was little real opposition to what I had to say. It was more a good natured scoffing, and a feeling that I was cracked a wee bit, perhaps, about the war.

I was not sorry to see New York again. We stayed there but one day, and then sailed for home on the Cunarder *Orduna* which has since been sunk, like many another good ship, by the Hun submarines.

But those were the days just before the Hun began his career of real frightfulness upon the sea – and under it. Even the Hun came gradually to the height of his powers in this war. It was not until some weeks later that he startled the world by proclaiming that every ship that dared to cross a certain zone of the sea would be sunk without warning.

When we sailed upon the old *Orduna* we had anxieties, to be sure. The danger of striking a mine was never absent, once we neared the British coasts. There was always the chance, we knew, that some German raider might have slipped through the cordon in the North Sea. But the terrors that were to follow the crime of the *Lusitania* still lay in the future. They were among the things no man could foresee.

The *Orduna* brought us safe to the Mersey and we landed at Liverpool. Even had there been no thought of danger to the ship, that voyage would have been a hard one for us to endure. We never ceased thinking of John, longing for him and news of him. It was near Christmas, but we had small hope that we should be able to see him on that day.

All through the voyage we were shut away from all news. The wireless is silenced in time of war, save for such work as the government allows. There is none of the free sending, from shore to ship, and ship to ship, of all the news of the world, such as one grows to welcome in time of peace. And so, from New York until we neared the British coast, we brooded, all of us. How fared it with Britain in the war? Had the Hun launched some new and terrible attack?

But two days out from home we saw a sight to make us glad and end our brooding for a space.

"Eh, Harry – come and look you!" someone called to me. It was early in the morning, and there was a mist about us.

I went to the rail and looked in the direction I was told. And there, rising suddenly out of the mist, shattering it, I saw great, gray ships – warships – British battleships and cruisers. There they were, some of the great ships that are the steel wall around Britain that holds her safe. My heart leaped with joy and pride at the sight of them, those great, gray guardians of the British shores, bulwarks of steel that fend all foemen from the rugged coast and the fair land that lies behind it.

Now we were safe, ourselves! Who would not trust the British navy, after the great deeds it has done in this war? For there, mind you, is the one force that has never failed. The British navy has done what it set out to do. It has kept command of the seas. The submarines? The tin fish? They do not command the sea! Have they kept Canada's men, and America's, from reaching France?

When we landed my first inquiry was for my son John. He was well, and he was still in England, in training at Bedford with his regiment, the Argyle and Sutherland Highlanders. But it was as we had feared. Our Christmas must be kept apart. And so the day before Christmas found us back in our wee hoose on the Clyde, at Dunoon. But we thought of little else but the laddie who was making ready to fight for us, and of the day, that was coming soon, when we should see him.

CHAPTER IV

It was a fitting place to train men for war, Bedford, where John was with his regiment, and where his mother and I went to see him so soon as we could after Christmas. It is in the British midlands, but before the factory towns begin. It is a pleasant, smiling country, farming country, mostly, with good roads, and fields that gave the boys chances to learn the work of digging trenches – aye, and living in them afterward.

Bedford is one of the great school towns of England. Low, rolling hills lie about it; the river Ouse, a wee, quiet stream, runs through it. Schooling must be in the air of Bedford! Three great schools for boys are there, and two for girls. And Liberty is in the air of Bedford, too, I think! John Bunyan was born two miles from Bedford, and his old house still stands in Elstow, a little village of old houses and great oaks. And it was in Bedford Jail that Bunyan was imprisoned because he would fight for the freedom of his own soul.

John was waiting to greet us, and he looked great. He had two stars now where he had one before – he had been promoted to first lieutenant. There were curious changes in the laddie I remembered. He was bigger, I thought, and he looked older, and graver. But that I could not wonder at. He had a great responsibility. The lives of other men had been entrusted to him, and John was not the man to take a responsibility like that lightly.

I saw him the first day I was at Bedford, leading some of his men in a practice charge. Big, braw laddies they were – all in their kilts. He ran ahead of them, smiling as he saw me watching them, but turning back to cheer them on if he thought they were not fast enough. I could see as I watched him that he had caught the habit of command. He was going to be a good officer. It was a proud thought for me, and again I was rejoiced that it was such a son that I was able to offer to my country.

They were kept busy at that training camp. Men were needed sore in France. Recruits were going over every day. What the retreat from Mons and the Battle of the Marne had left of that first heroic expeditionary force the first battle of Ypres had come close to wiping out. In the Ypres salient our men out there were hanging on like grim death. There was no time to spare at Bedford, where men were being made ready as quickly as might be to take their turn in the trenches.

But there was a little time when John and I could talk.

"What do you need most, son?" I asked him.

"Men!" he cried. "Men, Dad, men! They're coming in quickly. Oh, Britain has answered nobly to the call. But they're not coming in fast enough. We must have more men – more men!"

I had thought, when I asked my question, of something John might be needing for himself, or for his men, mayhap. But when he answered me so I said nothing. I only began to think. I wanted to go myself. But I knew they would not have me – yet awhile, at any rate. And still I felt that I must do something. I could not rest idle while all around me men were giving themselves and all they had and were.

Everywhere I heard the same cry that John had raised: "Men! Give us men!"

It came from Lord Kitchener. It came from the men in command in France and Belgium – that little strip of Belgium the Hun had not been able to conquer. It came from every broken, maimed man who came back home to Britain to be patched up that he might go out again. There were scores of thousands of men in Britain who needed only the last quick shove to send them across the line of enlistment. And after I had thought a while I hit upon a plan.

"What stirs a man's fighting spirit quicker or better than the right sort of music?" I asked myself. "And what sort of music does it best of all?"

There can be only one answer to that last question! And so I organized my recruiting band, that was to be famous all over Britain before so very long. I gathered fourteen of the best pipers and drummers I could find in all Scotland. I equipped them, gave them the Highland uniform, and sent them out, to travel over Britain skirling and drumming the wail of war through the length and breadth of the land. They were to go everywhere, carrying the shrieking of the pipes into the highways and the byways, and so they did. And I paid the bills.

That was the first of many recruiting bands that toured Britain. Because it was the first, and because of the way the pipers skirled out the old hill melodies and songs of Scotland, enormous crowds followed my band. And it led them straight to the recruiting stations. There was a swing and a sway about those old tunes that the young fellows couldn't resist.

The pipers would begin to skirl and the drums to beat in a square, maybe, or near the railway station. And every time the skirling of the pipes would bring the crowd. Then the pipers would march, when the crowd was big enough, and lead the way always to the recruiting place. And once they were there the young fellows who weren't "quite ready to decide" and the others who were just plain slackers, willing to let better men die for them, found it mighty hard to keep from going on the wee rest of the way that the pipers had left them to make alone!

It was wonderful work my band did, and when the returns came to me I felt like the Pied Piper! Yes I did, indeed!

I did not travel with my band. That would have been a waste of effort. There was work for both of us to do, separately. I was booked for a tour of Britain, and everywhere I went I spoke, and urged the young men to enlist. I made as many speeches as I could, in every town and city that I visited, and I made special trips to many. I thought, and there were those who agreed with me, that I could, it might be, reach audiences another speaker, better trained than I, no doubt, in this sort of work, would not touch.

So there was I, without official standing, going about, urging every man who could to don khaki. I talked wherever and whenever I could get an audience together, and I began then the habit of making speeches in the theatres, after my performance, that I have not yet given up. I talked thus to the young men.

"If you don't do your duty now," I told them, "you may live to be old men. But even if you do, you will regret it! Yours will be a sorrowful old age. In the years to come, mayhap, there'll be a wee grandchild nestling on your knee that'll circle its little arms about your neck and look into your wrinkled face, and ask you:

'How old are you, Grandpa? You're a very old man.'

"How will you answer that bairn's question?" So I asked the young men. And then I answered for them: "I don't know how old I am, but I am so old that I can remember the great war."

"And then" – I told them, the young men who were wavering – "and then will come the question that you will always have to dread – when you have won through to the old age that may be yours in safety if you shirk now! For the bairn will ask you, straightaway: 'Did – you – fight in the great war, Grandpa? What did you do?'

"God help the man," I told them, "who cannot hand it down as a heritage to his children and his children's children that he fought in the great war!"

I must have impressed many a brave lad who wanted only a bit of resolution to make him do his duty. They tell me that I and my band together influenced more than twelve thousand men to join the colors; they give me credit for that many, in one way and another. I am proud of that. But I am prouder still of the way the boys who enlisted upon my urging feel. Never a one has upbraided me; never a one has told me he was sorry he had heard me and been led to go.

It is far otherwise. The laddies who went because of me called me their godfather, many of them! Many's the letter I have had from them; many the one who has greeted me, as I was passing through a hospital, or, long afterward, when I made my first tour in France, behind the front line trenches. Many letters, did I say? I have had hundreds – thousands! And not so much as a word of regret in any one of them.

It was not only in Britain that I influenced enlistments. I preached the cause of the Empire in Canada, later. And here is a bit of verse that a Canadian sergeant sent to me. He dedicated it to me, indeed, and I am proud and glad that he did.

"ONE OF THE BOYS WHO WENT"

Say, here now, Mate,
Don't you figure it's great
To think when this war is all over;
When we're through with this mud,
And spilling o' blood,
And we're shipped back again to old Dover.
When they've paid us our tin,
And we've blown the lot in,

And our last penny is spent;
We'll still have a thought –
If it's all that we've got –
I'm one of the boys who went!
And perhaps later on
When your wild days are gone,
You'll be settling down for life,
You've a girl in your eye
You'll ask bye and bye
To share up with you as your wife.
When a few years have flown,
And you've kids of your own,
And you're feeling quite snug and content;
It'll make your heart glad
When they boast of their dad
As one of the boys who went!

There was much work for me to do beside my share in the campaign to increase enlistments. Every day now the wards of the hospitals were filling up. Men suffering from frightful wounds came back to be mended and made as near whole as might be. And among them there was work for me, if ever the world held work for any man.

I did not wait to begin my work in the hospitals. Everywhere I went, where there were wounded men, I sang for those who were strong enough to be allowed to listen, and told them stories, and did all I could to cheer them up. It was heartrending work, oftentimes. There were dour sights, dreadful sights in those hospitals. There were wounds the memory of which robbed me of sleep. There were men doomed to blindness for the rest of their lives.

But over all there was a spirit that never lagged or faltered, and that strengthened me when I thought some sight was more than I could bear. It was the spirit of the British soldier, triumphant over suffering and cruel disfigurement, with his inevitable answer to any question as to how he was getting on. I never heard that answer varied when a man could speak at all. Always it was the same. Two words were enough.

"All right!"

CHAPTER V

As I went about the country now, working hard to recruit men, to induce people to subscribe to the war loan, doing all the things in which I saw a chance to make myself useful, there was now an ever present thought. When would John go out? He must soon. I knew that, so did his mother. We had learned that he would not be sent without a chance to bid us good-by. There we were better off than many a father and mother in the early days of the war. Many's the mother who learned first that her lad had gone to France when they told her he was dead. And many's the lassie who learned in the same way that her lover would never come home to be her husband.

But by now Britain was settled down to war. It was as if war were the natural state of things, and everything was adjusted to war and those who must fight it. And many things were ordered better and more mercifully than they had been at first.

It was in April that word came to us. We might see John again, his mother and I, if we hurried to Bedford. And so we did. For once I heeded no other call. It was a sad journey, but I was proud and glad as well as sorry. John must do his share. There was no reason why my son should take fewer risks than another man's. That was something all Britain was learning in those days. We were one people. We must fight as one; one for all – all for one.

John was sober when he met us. Sober, aye! But what a light there was in his eyes! He was eager to be at the Huns. Tales of their doings were coming back to us now, faster and faster. They were tales to shock me. But they were tales, too, to whet the courage and sharpen the steel of every man who could fight and meant to go.

It was John's turn to go. So it was he felt. And so it was his mother and I bid him farewell, there at Bedford. We did not know whether we would ever see him again, the bonnie laddie! We had to bid him good-by, lest it be our last chance. For in Britain we knew, by then, what were the chances they took, those boys of ours who went out.

"Good-by, son – good luck!"

"Good-by, Dad. See you when I get leave!"

That was all. We were not allowed to know more than that he was ordered to France. Whereabouts in the long trench line he would be sent we were not told. "Somewhere in France." That phrase, that had been dinned so often into our ears, had a meaning for us now.

And now, indeed, our days and nights were anxious ones. The war was in our house as it had never been before. I could think of nothing but my boy. And yet, all the time I had to go on. I had to carry on, as John was always bidding his men do. I had to appear daily before my audiences, and laugh and sing, that I might make them laugh, and so be better able to do their part.

They had made me understand, my friends, by that time, that it was really right for me to carry on with my own work. I had not thought so at first. I had felt that it was wrong for me to be singing at such a time. But they showed me that I was influencing thousands to do their duty, in one way or another, and that I was helping to keep up the spirit of Britain, too.

"Never forget the part that plays, Harry," my friends told me. "That's the thing the Hun can't understand. He thought the British would be poor fighters because they went into action with a laugh. But that's the thing that makes them invincible. You've your part to do in keeping up that spirit."

So I went on but it was with a heavy heart, oftentimes. John's letters were not what made my heart heavy. There was good cheer in everyone of them. He told us as much as the censor's rules would let him of the front, and of conditions as he found them. They were still bad – cruelly bad. But there was no word of complaint from John.

The Germans still had the best of us in guns in those days, although we were beginning to catch up with them. And they knew more about making themselves comfortable in the trenches than did our boys. No wonder! They spent years of planning and making ready for this war. And it has not taken us so long, all things considered, to catch up with them.

John's letters were cheery and they came regularly, too, for a time. But I suppose it was because they left out so much, because there was so great a part of my boy's life that was hidden from me, that I found myself thinking more and more of John as a wee bairn and as a lad growing up.

He was a real boy. He had the real boy's spirit of fun and mischief. There was a story I had often told of him that came to my mind now. We were living in Glasgow. One drizzly day, Mrs. Lauder kept John in the house, and he spent the time standing at the parlor window looking down on the street, apparently innocently interested in the passing traffic.

In Glasgow it is the custom for the coal dealers to go along the streets with their lorries, crying their wares, much after the manner of a vegetable peddler in America. If a housewife wants any coal, she goes to the window when she hears the hail of the coal man, and holds up a finger, or two fingers, according to the number of sacks of coal she wants.

To Mrs. Lauder's surprise, and finally to her great vexation, coal men came tramping up our stairs every few minutes all afternoon, each one staggering under the weight of a hundredweight sack of coal. She had ordered no coal and she wanted no coal, but still the coal men came – a veritable pest of them.

They kept coming, too, until she discovered that little John was the author of their grimy pilgrimages to our door. He was signalling every passing lorrie from the window in the Glasgow coal code!

I watched him from that window another day when he was quarreling with a number of playmates in the street below. The quarrel finally ended in a fight. John was giving one lad a pretty good pegging, when the others decided that the battle was too much his way, and jumped on him.

John promptly executed a strategic retreat. He retreated with considerable speed, too. I saw him running; I heard the patter of his feet on our stairs, and a banging at our door. I opened it and admitted a flushed, disheveled little warrior, and I heard the other boys shouting up the stairs what they would do to him.

By the time I got the door closed, and got back to our little parlor, John was standing at the window, giving a marvelous pantomime for the benefit of his enemies in the street. He was putting his small, clenched fist now to his nose, and now to his jaw, to indicate to the youngsters what he was going to do to them later on.

Those, and a hundred other little incidents, were as fresh in my memory as if they had only occurred yesterday. His mother and I recalled them over and over again. From the day John was born, it seems to me the only things that really interested me were the things in which he was concerned. I used to tuck him in his crib at night. The affairs of his babyhood were far more important to me than my own personal affairs.

I watched him grow and develop with enormous pride, and he took great pride in me. That to me was far sweeter than praise from crowned heads. Soon he was my constant companion. He was my business confidant. More – he was my most intimate friend.

There were no secrets between us. I think that John and I talked of things that few fathers and sons have the courage to discuss. He never feared to ask my advice on any subject, and I never feared to give it to him.

I wish you could have known my son as he was to me. I wish all fathers could know their sons as I knew John. He was the most brilliant conversationalist I have ever known. He was my ideal musician.

He took up music only as an accomplishment, however. He did not want to be a performer, although he had amazing natural talent in that direction. Music was born in him. He could transpose a melody in any key. You could whistle an air for him, and he could turn it into a little opera at once.

However, he was anxious to make for himself in some other line of endeavor, and while he was often my piano accompanist, he never had any intention of going on the stage.

When he was fifteen years old, I was commanded to appear before King Edward, who was a guest at Rufford Abbey, the seat of Lord and Lady Sayville, situated in a district called the Dukeries, and I took John as my accompanist.

I gave my usual performance, and while I was making my changes, John played the piano. At the close, King Edward sent for me, and thanked me. It was a proud moment for me, but a prouder moment came when the King spoke of John's playing, and thanked him for his part in the entertainment.

There were curious contradictions, it often seemed to me, in John. His uncle, Tom Vallance, was in his day, one of the very greatest football players in Scotland. But John never greatly liked the game. He thought it was too rough. He thought any game was a poor game in which players were likely to be hurt. And yet – he had been eager for the rough game of war! The roughest game of all! Ah, but that was not a game to him! He was not one of those who went to war with a light heart, as they might have entered upon a football match. All honor to those who went into the war so – they played a great part and a noble part! But there were more who went to war as my boy did – taking it upon themselves as a duty and a solemn obligation. They had no illusions. They did not love war. No! John hated war, and the black ugly horrors of it. But there were things he hated more than he hated war. And one was a peace won through submission to injustice.

Have I told you how my boy looked? He was slender, but he was strong and wiry. He was about five feet five inches tall; he topped his Dad by a handspan. And he was the neatest boy you might ever have hoped to see. Aye – but he did not inherit that from me! Indeed, he used to reproach me, oftentimes, for being careless about my clothes. My collar would be loose, perhaps, or my waistcoat would not fit just so. He'd not like that, and he would tell me so!

When he did that I would tell him of times when he was a wee boy, and would come in from play with a dirty face; how his mother would order him to wash, and how he would painstakingly mop off just enough of his features to leave a dark ring abaft his cheeks, and above his eyes, and below his chin.

"You wash your face, but never let on to your neck," I would tell him when he was a wee laddie.

He had a habit then of parting and brushing about an inch of his hair, leaving the rest all topsy-turvy. My recollection of that boyhood habit served me as a defense in later years when he would call my attention to my own disordered hair.

I linger long, and I linger lovingly over these small details, because they are part of my daily thoughts. Every day some little incident comes up to remind me of my boy. A battered old hamper, in which I carry my different character make-ups, stands in my dressing room. It was John's favorite seat. Every time I look at it I have a vision of a tiny wide-eyed boy perched on the lid, watching me make ready for the stage. A lump rises, unbidden, in my throat.

In all his life, I never had to admonish my son once. Not once. He was the most considerate lad I have ever known. He was always thinking of others. He was always doing for others.

It was with such thoughts as these that John's mother and I filled in the time between his letters. They came as if by a schedule. We knew what post should bring one. And once or twice a letter was a post late and our hearts were in our throats with fear. And then came a day when there should have been a letter, and none came. The whole day passed. I tried to comfort John's mother! I tried to believe myself that it was no more than a mischance of the post. But it was not that.

We could do nought but wait. Ah, but the folks at home in Britain know all too well those sinister breaks in the chains of letters from the front! Such a break may mean nothing or anything.

For us, news came quickly. But it was not a letter from John that came to us. It was a telegram from the war office and it told us no more than that our boy was wounded and in hospital.

CHAPTER VI

"Wounded and in hospital!"

That might have meant anything. And for a whole week that was all we knew. To hope for word more definite until – and unless – John himself could send us a message, appeared to be hopeless. Every effort we made ended in failure. And, indeed, at such a time, private inquiries could not well be made. The messages that had to do with the war and with the business of the armies had to be dealt with first.

But at last, after a week in which his mother and I almost went mad with anxiety, there came a note from our laddie himself. He told us not to fret – that all that ailed him was that his nose was split and his wrist bashed up a bit! His mother looked at me and I at her. It seemed bad enough to us! But he made light of his wounds – aye, and he was right! When I thought of men I'd seen in hospitals – men with wounds so frightful that they may not be told of – I rejoiced that John had fared so well.

And I hoped, too, that his wounds would bring him home to us – to Blighty, as the Tommies were beginning to call Britain. But his wounds were not serious enough for that and so soon as they were healed, he went back to the trenches.

"Don't worry about me," he wrote to us. "Lots of fellows out here have been wounded five and six times, and don't think anything of it. I'll be all right so long as I don't get knocked out."

He didn't tell us then that it was the bursting of a shell that gave him his first wounded stripe. But he wrote to us regularly again, and there were scarcely any days in which a letter did not come either to me or to his mother. When one of those breaks did come it was doubly hard to bear now.

For now we knew what it was to dread the sight of a telegraph messenger. Few homes in Britain there are that do not share that knowledge now. It is by telegraph, from the war office, that bad news comes first. And so, with the memory of that first telegram that we had had, matters were even worse, somehow, than they had been before. For me the days and nights dragged by as if they would never pass.

There was more news in John's letters now. We took some comfort from that. I remember one in which he told his mother how good a bed he had finally made for himself the night before. For some reason he was without quarters – either a billet or a dug-out. He had to skirmish around, for he did not care to sleep simply in Flanders mud. But at last he found two handfuls of straw, and with them made his couch.

"I got a good two hours' sleep," he wrote to his mother. "And I was perfectly comfortable. I can tell you one thing, too, Mother. If I ever get home after this experience, there'll be one in the house who'll never grumble! This business puts the grumbling out of your head. This is where the men are. This is where every man ought to be."

In another letter he told us that nine of his men had been killed.

"We buried them last night," he wrote, "just as the sun went down. It was the first funeral I have ever attended. It was most impressive. We carried the boys to one huge grave. The padre said a prayer, and we lowered the boys into the ground, and we all sang a little hymn: 'Peace, Perfect Peace!' Then I called my men to attention again, and we marched straight back into the trenches, each of us, I dare say, wondering who would be the next."

John was promoted for the second time in Flanders. He was a captain, having got his step on the field of battle. Promotion came swiftly in those days to those who proved themselves worthy. And all of the few reports that came to us of John showed us that he was a good officer. His men liked him, and trusted him, and would follow him anywhere. And little more than that can be said of any officer.

While Captain John Lauder was playing his part across the Channel, I was still trying to do what I could at home. My band still travelled up and down, the length and width of the United Kingdom, skirling and drumming and drawing men by the score to the recruiting office.

There was no more talk now of a short war. We knew what we were in for now.

But there was no thought or talk of anything save victory. Let the war go on as long as it must – it could end only in one way. We had been forced into the fight – but we were in, and we were in to stay. John, writing from France, was no more determined than those at home.

It was not very long before there came again a break in John's letters. We were used to the days – far apart – that brought no word. Not until the second day and the third day passed without a word, did Mrs. Lauder and I confess our terrors and our anxiety to ourselves and one another. This time our suspense was comparatively short-lived. Word came that John was in hospital again – at the Duke of Westminster's hospital at Le Toquet, in France. This time he was not wounded; he was suffering from dysentery, fever and – a nervous breakdown. That was what staggered his mother and me. A nervous breakdown! We could not reconcile the John we knew with the idea that the words conveyed to us. He had been high strung, to be sure, and sensitive. But never had he been the sort of boy of whom to expect a breakdown so severe as this must be if they had sent him to the hospital.

We could only wait to hear from him, however. And it was several weeks before he was strong enough to be able to write to us. There was no hint of discouragement in what he wrote then. On the contrary, he kept on trying to reassure us, and if he ever grew downhearted, he made it his business to see that we did not suspect it. Here is one of his letters – like most of them it was not about himself.

"I had a sad experience yesterday," he wrote to me. "It was the first day I was able to be out of bed, and I went over to a piano in a corner against the wall, sat down, and began playing very softly, more to myself than anything else.

"One of the nurses came to me, and said a Captain Webster, of the Gordon Highlanders, who lay on a bed in the same ward, wanted to speak to me. She said he had asked who was playing, and she had told him Captain Lauder – Harry Lauder's son. 'Oh,' he said, 'I know Harry Lauder very well. Ask Captain Lauder to come here?'

"This man had gone through ten operations in less than a week. I thought perhaps my playing had disturbed him, but when I went to his bedside, he grasped my hand, pressed it with what little strength he had left, and thanked me. He asked me if I could play a hymn. He said he would like to hear 'Lead, Kindly Light.'

"So I went back to the piano and played it as softly and as gently as I could. It was his last request. He died an hour later. I was very glad I was able to soothe his last moments a little. I am very glad now I learned the hymn at Sunday School as a boy."

Soon after we received that letter there came what we could not but think great news. John was ordered home! He was invalided, to be sure, and I warned his mother that she must be prepared for a shock when she saw him. But no matter how ill he was, we would have our lad with us for a space. And for that much British fathers and mothers had learned to be grateful.

I had warned John's mother, but it was I who was shocked when I saw him first on the day he came back to our wee hoose at Dunoon. His cheeks were sunken, his eyes very bright, as a man's are who has a fever. He was weak and thin, and there was no blood in his cheeks. It was a sight to wring one's heart to see the laddie so brought down – him who had looked so braw and strong the last time we had seen him.

That had been when he was setting out for the wars, you ken! And now he was back, sae thin and weak and pitiful as I had not seen him since he had been a bairn in his mother's arms.

Aweel, it was for us, his mother and I, and all the folks at home, to mend him, and make him strong again. So he told us, for he had but one thing on his mind – to get back to his men.

"They'll be needing me, out there," he said. "They're needing men. I must go back so soon as I can. Every man is needed there."

"You'll be needing your strength back before you can be going back, son," I told him. "If you fash and fret it will take you but so much the longer to get back."

He knew that. But he knew things I could not know, because I had not seen them. He had seen things that he saw over and over again when he tried to sleep. His nerves were shattered utterly. It grieved me sore not to spend all my time with him but he would not hear of it. He drove me back to my work.

"You must work on, Dad, like every other Briton," he said. "Think of the part you're playing. Why you're more use than any of us out there – you're worth a brigade!"

So I left him on the Clyde, and went on about my work. But I went back to Dunoon as often as I could, as

I got a day or a night to make the journey. At first there was small change of progress. John would come downstairs about the middle of the day, moving slowly and painfully. And he was listless; there was no life in him; no resiliency or spring.

"How did you rest, son?" I would ask him. He always smiled when he answered.

"Oh, fairly well," he'd tell me. "I fought three or four battles though, before I dropped off to sleep."

He had come to the right place to be cured, though, and his mother was the nurse he needed. It was quiet in the hills of the Clyde, and there was rest and healing in the heather about Dunoon. Soon his sleep became better and less troubled by dreams. He could eat more, too, and they saw to it, at home, that he ate all they could stuff into him.

So it was a surprisingly short time, considering how bad he had looked when he first came back to Dunoon, before he was in good health and spirits again. There was a bonnie, wee lassie who was to become Mrs. John Lauder ere so long – she helped our boy, too, to get back his strength.

Soon he was ordered from home. For a time he had only light duties with the Home Reserve. Then he went to school. I laughed when he told me he had been ordered to school, but he didna crack a smile.

"You needn't be laughing," he said. "It's a bombing school I'm going to now-a-days. If you're away from the front for a few weeks, you find everything changed when you get back. Bombing is going to be important."

John did so well in the bombing school that he was made an instructor and assigned, for a while, to teach others. But he was impatient to be back with his own men, and they were clamoring for him. And so, on September 16, 1916, his mother and I bade him good-by again, and he went back to France and the men his heart was wrapped up in.

"Yon's where the men are, Dad!" he said to me, just before he started.

CHAPTER VII

John's mother, his sweetheart and I all saw him off at Glasgow. The fear was in all our hearts, and I think it must have been in all our eyes, as well – the fear that every father and mother and sweetheart in Britain shared with us in these days whenever they saw a boy off for France and the trenches. Was it for the last time? Were we seeing him now so strong and hale and hearty, only to have to go the rest of our lives with no more than a memory of him to keep?

Aweel, we could not be telling that! We could only hope and pray! And we had learned again to pray, long since. I have wondered, often, and Mrs. Lauder has wondered with me, what the fathers and mothers of Britain would do in these black days without prayer to guide them and sustain them. So we could but stand there, keeping back our tears and our fears, and hoping for the best. One thing was sure; we might not let the laddie see how close we were to greeting. It was for us to be so brave as God would let us be. It was hard for him. He was no boy, you ken, going blindly and gayly to a great adventure; he had need of the finest courage and devotion a man could muster that day.

For he knew fully now what it was that he was going back to. He knew the hell the Huns had made of war, which had been bad enough, in all conscience, before they did their part to make it worse. And he was high strung. He could live over, and I make no doubt he did, in those days after he had his orders to go back, every grim and dreadful thing that was waiting for him out there. He had been through it all, and he was going back. He had come out of the valley of the shadow, and now he was to ride down into it again.

And it was with a smile he left us! I shall never forget that. His thought was all for us whom he was leaving behind. His care was for us, lest we should worry too greatly and think too much of him.

"I'll be all right," he told us. "You're not to fret about me, any of you. A man does take his chances out there – but they're the chances every man must take these days, if he's a man at all. I'd rather be taking them than be safe at home."

We did our best to match the laddie's spirit and be worthy of him. But it was cruelly hard. We had lost him and found him again, and now he was being taken from us for the second time. It was harder, much harder, to see him go this second time than it had been at first, and it had been hard enough then, and bad enough. But there was nothing else for it. So much we knew. It was a thing ordered and inevitable.

And it was not many days before we had slipped back into the way things had been before John was invalided home. It is a strange thing about life, the way that one can become used to things. So it was with us. Strange things, terrible things, outrageous things, that, in time of peace, we would never have dared so much as to think possible, came to be the matters of every day for us. It was so with John. We came to think of it as natural that he should be away from us, and in peril of his life every minute of every hour. It was not easier for us. Indeed, it was harder than it had been before, just as it had been harder for us to say good-by the second time. But we thought less often of the strangeness of it. We were really growing used to the war, and it was less the monstrous, strange thing than it had been in our daily lives. War had become our daily life and portion in Britain. All who were not slackers were doing their part – every one. Man and woman and child were in it, making sacrifices. Those happy days of peace lay far behind us, and we had lost our touch with them and our memory of them was growing dim. We were all in it. We had all to suffer alike, we were all in the same boat, we mothers and fathers and sweethearts of Britain. And so it was easier for us not to think too much and too often of our own griefs and cares and anxieties.

John's letters began to come again in a steady stream. He was as careful as ever about writing. There was scarcely a day that did not bring its letter to one of the three of us. And what bonnie, brave letters they were! They were as cheerful and as bright as his first letters had been. If John had bad hours and bad days out there he would not let us know it. He told us what news there was, and he was always cheerful and bright when he wrote. He let no hint of discouragement creep into anything he wrote to us. He thought of others first, always and all the time; of his men, and of us at home. He was quite cured and well, he told us, and going back had done him good instead of harm. He wrote to us that he felt as if he had come home. He felt, you ken, that it was there, in France and in the trenches, that men should feel at home in those days, and not safe in Britain by their ain firesides.

It was not easy for me to be cheerful and comfortable about him, though. I had my work to do. I tried to do it as well as I could, for I knew that that would please him. My band still went up and down the country, getting recruits, and I was speaking, too, and urging men myself to go out and join the lads who were fighting and dying for them in France. They told me I was doing good work; that I was a great force in the war. And I did, indeed, get many a word and many a handshake from men who told me I had induced them to enlist.

"I'm glad I heard you, Harry," man after man said to me. "You showed me what I should be doing and I've been easier in my mind ever since I put on the khaki!"

I knew they'd never regret it, no matter what came to them. No man will, that's done his duty. It's the slackers who couldn't or wouldn't see their duty men should feel sorry for! It's not the lads who gave everything and made the final sacrifice.

It was hard for me to go on with my work of making folks laugh. It had been growing harder steadily ever since I had come home from America and that long voyage of mine to Australia and had seen what war was and what it was doing to Britain. But I carried on, and did the best I could.

That winter I was in the big revue at the Shaftesbury Theatre, in London, that was called "Three Cheers." It was one of the gay shows that London liked because it gave some relief from the war and made the Zeppelin raids that the Huns were beginning to make so often now a little easier to bear. And it was a great place for the men who were back from France. It was partly because of them that I could go on as I did. We owed them all we could give them. And when they came back from the mud and the grime and the dreariness of the trenches, they needed something to cheer them up – needed the sort of production we gave them. A man who has two days' leave in London does not want to see a serious play or a problem drama, as a rule. He wants something light, with lots of pretty girls and jolly tunes and people to make him laugh. And we gave him that. The house was full of officers and men, night after night.

Soon word came from John that he was to have leave, just after Christmas, that would bring him home for the New Year's holidays. His mother went home to make things ready, for John was to be married when he got his leave. I had my plans all made. I meant to build a wee hoose for the two of them, near our own hoose at Dunoon, so that we might be all together, even though my laddie was in a home of his own. And I counted the hours and the days against the time when John would be home again.

While we were playing at the Shaftesbury I lived at an hotel in Southampton Row called the Bonnington.

But it was lonely for me there. On New Year's Eve – it fell on a Sunday – Tom Vallance, my brother-in-law, asked me to tea with him and his family in Clapham, where he lived. That is a pleasant place, a suburb of London on the southwest, and I was glad to go. And so I drove out with a friend of mine, in a taxicab, and was glad to get out of the crowded part of the city for a time.

I did not feel right that day. Holiday times were bad, hard times for me then. We had always made so much of Christmas, and here was the third Christmas that our boy had been away. And so I was depressed. And then, there had been no word for me from John for a day or two. I was not worried, for I thought it likely that his mother or his sweetheart had heard, and had not time yet to let me know. But, whatever the reason, I was depressed and blue, and I could not enter into the festive spirit that folk were trying to keep alive despite the war.

I must have been poor company during that ride to Clapham in the taxicab. We scarcely exchanged a word, my friend and I. I did not feel like talking, and he respected my mood, and kept quiet himself. I felt, at last, that I ought to apologize to him.

"I don't know what's the matter with me," I told him. "I simply don't want to talk. I feel sad and lonely. I wonder if my boy is all right?"

"Of course he is!" my friend told me. "Cheer up, Harry. This is a time when no news is good news. If anything were wrong with him they'd let you know."

Well, I knew that, too. And I tried to cheer up, and feel better, so that I would not spoil the pleasure of the others at Tom Vallance's house. I tried to picture

John as I thought he must be – well, and happy, and smiling the old, familiar boyish smile I knew so well. I had sent him a box of cigars only a few days before, and he would be handing it around among his fellow officers. I knew that! But it was no use. I could think of John, but it was only with sorrow and longing. And I wondered if this same time in a year would see him still out there, in the trenches. Would this war ever end? And so the shadows still hung about me when we reached Tom's house.

They made me very welcome, did Tom and all his family. They tried to cheer me, and Tom did all he could to make me feel better, and to reassure me. But I was still depressed when we left the house and began the drive back to London.

"It's the holiday – I'm out of gear with that, I'm thinking," I told my friend.

He was going to join two other friends, and, with them, to see the New Year in in an old fashioned way, and he wanted me to join them. But I did not feel up to it; I was not in the mood for anything of the sort.

"No, no, I'll go home and turn in," I told him. "I'm too dull tonight to be good company."

He hoped, as we all did, that this New Year that was coming would bring victory and peace. Peace could not come without victory; we were all agreed on that. But we all hoped that the New Year would bring both – the new year of 1917. And so I left him at the corner of Southampton Row, and went back to my hotel alone. It was about midnight, a little before, I think, when I got in, and one of the porters had a message for me.

"Sir Thomas Lipton rang you up," he said, "and wants you to speak with him when you come in."

I rang him up at home directly.

"Happy New Year, when it comes, Harry!" he said. He spoke in the same bluff, hearty way he always did. He fairly shouted in my ear. "When did you hear from the boy? Are you and Mrs. Lauder well?"

"Aye, fine," I told him. And I told him my last news of John.

"Splendid!" he said. "Well, it was just to talk to you a minute that I rang you up, Harry. Good-night – Happy New Year again."

I went to bed then. But I did not go to sleep for a long time. It was New Year's, and I lay thinking of my boy, and wondering what this year would bring him. It was early in the morning before I slept. And it seemed to me that I had scarce been asleep at all when there came a pounding at the door, loud enough to rouse the heaviest sleeper there ever was.

My heart almost stopped. There must be something serious indeed for them to be rousing me so early. I rushed to the door, and there was a porter, holding out a telegram. I took it and tore it open. And I knew why I had felt as I had the day before. I shall never forget what I read:

"Captain John Lauder killed in action, December 28. Official. War Office."

It had gone to Mrs. Lauder at Dunoon first, and she had sent it on to me. That was all it said. I knew nothing of how my boy had died, or where – save that it was for his country.

But later I learned that when Sir Thomas Lipton had rung me up he had intended to condole with me. He had heard on Saturday of my boy's death. But when he spoke to me, and understood at once, from the tone of my voice, that I did not know, he had not been able to go on. His heart was too tender to make it possible for him to be the one to give me that blow – the heaviest that ever befell me.

CHAPTER VIII

It was on Monday morning, January the first, 1917, that I learned of my boy's death. And he had been killed the Thursday before! He had been dead four days before I knew it! And yet – I had known. Let no one ever tell me again that there is nothing in presentiment. Why else had I been so sad and uneasy in my mind? Why else, all through that Sunday, had it been so impossible for me to take comfort in what was said to cheer me? Some warning had come to me, some sense that all was not well.

Realization came to me slowly. I sat and stared at that slip of paper, that had come to me like the breath of doom. Dead! Dead these four days! I was never to see the light of his eyes again. I was never to hear that laugh of his. I had looked on my boy for the last time. Could it be true? Ah, I knew it was! And it was for this moment that I had been waiting, that we had all been waiting, ever since we had sent John away to fight for his country and do his part. I think we had all felt that it must come. We had all known that it was too much to hope that he should be one of those to be spared.

The black despair that had been hovering over me for hours closed down now and enveloped all my senses. Everything was unreal. For a time I was quite numb. But then, as I began to realize and to visualize what it was to mean in my life that my boy was dead there came a great pain. The iron of realization slowly seared every word of that curt telegram upon my heart. I said it to myself, over and over again. And I whispered to myself, as my thoughts took form, over and over, the one terrible word: "Dead!"

I felt that for me everything had come to an end with the reading of that dire message. It seemed to me that for me the board of life was black and blank. For me there was no past and there could be no future. Everything had been swept away, erased, by one sweep of the hand of a cruel fate. Oh, there was a past, though! And it was in that past that I began to delve. It was made up of every memory I had of my boy. I fell at once to remembering him. I clutched at every memory, as if I must grasp them and make sure of them, lest they be taken from me as well as the hope of seeing him again that the telegram had forever snatched away.

I would have been destitute indeed then. It was as if I must fix in my mind the way he had been wont to look, and recall to my ears every tone of his voice, every trick of his speech. There was something left of him that I must keep, I knew, even then, at all costs, if I was to be able to bear his loss at all.

There was a vision of him before my eyes. My bonnie Highland laddie, brave and strong in his kilt and the uniform of his country, going out to his death with a smile on his face. And there was another vision that came up now, unbidden. It was a vision of him lying stark and cold upon the battlefield, the mud on his uniform. And when I saw that vision I was like a man gone mad and possessed of devils who had stolen away his faculties. I cursed war as I saw that vision, and the men who caused war. And when I thought of the Germans who had killed my boy a terrible and savage hatred swept me, and I longed to go out there and kill with my bare hands until I had avenged him or they had killed me too.

But then I was a little softened. I thought of his mother back in our wee hoose at Dunoon. And the thought of her, bereft even as I was, sorrowing, even as I was, and lost in her frightful loneliness, was pitiful, so that I had but the one desire and wish – to go to her, and join my tears with hers, that we who were left alone to bear our grief might bear it together and give one to the other such comfort as there might be in life for us. And so I fell upon my knees and prayed, there in my lonely room in the hotel. I prayed to God that he might give us both, John's mother and myself, strength to bear the blow that had been dealt us and to endure the sacrifice that He and our country had demanded of us.

My friends came to me. They came rushing to me. Never did man have better friends, and kindlier friends than mine proved themselves to me on that day of sorrow. They did all that good men and women could do.

But there was no help for me in the ministration of friends. I was beyond the power of human words to comfort or solace. I was glad of their kindness, and the memory of it now is a precious one, and one I would not be without. But at such a time I could not gain from them what they were eager to give me. I could only bow my head and pray for strength.

That night, that New Year's night that I shall never forget, no matter how long God may let me live, I went north. I took the train from London to Glasgow, and the next day I came to our wee hoose – a sad, lonely wee hoose it had become now! – on the Clyde at Dunoon, and was with John's mother. It was the place for me. It was there that I wanted to be, and it was with her, who must hereafter be all the world to me. And I was eager to be with her, too, who had given John to me. Sore as my grief was, stricken as I was, I could comfort her as no one else could hope to do, and she could do as much for me. We belonged together.

I can scarce remember, even for myself, what happened there at Dunoon. I cannot tell you what I said or what I did, or what words and what thoughts passed between John's mother and myself. But there are some things that I do know and that I will tell you.

Almighty God, to whom we prayed, was kind, and He was pitiful and merciful. For presently He brought us both a sort of sad composure. Presently He assuaged our grief a little, and gave us the strength that we must have to meet the needs of life and the thought of going on in a world that was darkened by the loss of the boy in whom all our thoughts and all our hopes had been centred. I thanked God then, and I thank God now, that I have never denied Him nor taken His name in vain.

For God gave me great thoughts about my boy and about his death. Slowly, gradually, He made me to see things in their true light, and He took away the sharp agony of my first grief and sorrow, and gave me a sort of peace.

John died in the most glorious cause, and he died the most glorious death, it may be given to a man to die. He died for humanity. He died for liberty, and that this world in which life must go on, no matter how many die, may be a better world to live in. He died in a struggle against the blackest force and the direst threat that has appeared against liberty and humanity within the memory of man. And were he alive now, and were he called again to-day to go out for the same cause, knowing that he must meet death – as he did meet it – he would go as smilingly and as willingly as he went then. He would go as a British soldier and a British gentleman, to fight and die for his King and his country. And I would bid him go.

I have lived through much since his death. They have not let me take a rifle or a sword and go into the trenches to avenge him. . . . But of that I shall tell you later.

Ah, it was not at once that I felt so! In my heart, in those early days of grief and sorrow, there was rebellion, often and often. There were moments when in my anguish I cried out, aloud: "Why? Why? Why did they have to take John, my boy – my only child?"

But God came to me, and slowly His peace entered my soul. And He made me see, as in a vision, that some things that I had said and that I had believed, were not so. He made me know, and I learned, straight from Him, that our boy had not been taken from us forever as I had said to myself so often since that telegram had come.

He is gone from this life, but he is waiting for us beyond this life. He is waiting beyond this life and this world of wicked war and wanton cruelty and slaughter. And we shall come, some day, his mother and I, to the place where he is waiting for us, and we shall all be as happy there as we were on this earth in the happy days before the war.

My eyes will rest again upon his face. I will hear his fresh young voice again as he sees me and cries out his greeting. I know what he will say. He will spy me, and his voice will ring out as it used to do. "Hello, Dad!" he will call, as he sees me. And I will feel the grip of his young, strong arms about me, just as in the happy days before that day that is of all the days of my life the most terrible and the most hateful in my memory – the day when they told me that he had been killed.

That is my belief. That is the comfort that God has given me in my grief and my sorrow. There is a God. Ah, yes, there is a God! Times there are, I know, when some of those who look upon the horrid slaughter of this war, that is going on, hour by hour, feel that their faith is being shaken by doubts. They think of the sacrifices, of the blood that is being poured out, of the sufferings of women and children. And they see the cause that is wrong and foul prospering, for a little time, and they cannot understand.

"If there is a God," they whisper to themselves, "why does he permit a thing so wicked to go on?"

But there is a God – there is! I have seen the stark horror of war. I know, as none can know until he has seen it at close quarters, what a thing war is as it is fought to-day. And I believe as I do believe, and as I shall believe until the end, because I know God's comfort and His grace. I know that my boy is surely waiting for me. In America, now, there are mothers and fathers by the scores of thousands who have bidden their sons good-by; who water their letters from France with their tears – who turn white at the sight of a telegram and tremble at the sudden clamor of a telephone. Ah, I know – I know! I suffered as they are suffering! And I have this to tell them and to beg them. They must believe as I believe – then shall they find the peace and the comfort that I have found.

So it was that there, on the Clyde, John's mother and I came out of the blackness of our first grief. We began to be able to talk to one another. And every day we talked of John. We have never ceased to do that, his mother and I. We never shall. We may not have him with us bodily, but his spirit is never absent. And each day we remember some new thing about him that one of us can call to the other's mind. And it is as if, when we do that, we bring back some part of him out of the void.

Little, trifling memories of when he was a baby, and when he was a boy, growing up! And other memories, of later days. Often and often it was the days that were furthest away that we remembered best of all, and things connected with those days.

But I had small wish to see others. John's mother was enough for me. She and the peace that was coming to me on the Clyde. I could not bear to think of London. I had no plans to make. All that was over. All that part of my life, I thought, had ended with the news of my boy's death. I wanted no more than to stay at home on the Clyde and think of him. My wife and I did not even talk about the future. And no thing was further from all my thoughts than that I should ever step upon a stage again.

What! Go out before an audience and seek to make it laugh? Sing my songs when my heart was broken? I did not decide not to do it. I did not so much as think of it as a thing I had to decide about.

CHAPTER IX

And then one thing and another brought the thought into my mind, so that I had to face it and tell people how I felt about it. There were neighbors, wanting to know when I would be about my work again. That it was that first made me understand that others did not feel as I was feeling.

"They're thinking I'll be going back to work again," I told John's mother. "I canna'!"

She felt as I did. We could not see, either one of us, in our grief, how anyone could think that I could begin again where I had left off.

"I canna'! I will not try!" I told her, again and again. "How can I tak up again with that old mummery? How can I laugh when my heart is breaking, and make others smile when the tears are in my eyes?"

And she thought as I did, that I could not, and that no one should be asking me. The war had taken much of what I had earned, in one way or another. I was not so rich as I had been, but there was enough. There was no need for me to go back to work, so far as our living was concerned. And so it seemed to be settled between us. Planning we left for the future. It was no time for us to be making plans. It mattered little enough to us what might be in store for us. We could take things as they might come.

So we bided quiet in our home, and talked of John. And from every part of the earth and from people in all walks and conditions of life there began to pour in upon us letters and telegrams of sympathy and sorrow. I think there were four thousand kindly folk who remembered us in our sorrow, and let us know that they could think of us in spite of all the other care and trouble that filled the world in those days. Many celebrated names were signed to those letters and telegrams, and there were many, too, from simple folk whose very names I did not know, who told me that I had given them cheer and courage from the stage, and so they felt that they were friends of mine, and must let me know that they were sorry for the blow that had befallen me.

Then it came out that I meant to leave the stage. They sent word from London, at last, to ask when they might look for me to be back at the Shaftesbury Theatre. And when they found what it was in my mind to do all my friends began to plead with me and argue with me. They said it was my duty to myself to go back.

"You're too young a man to retire, Harry," they said. "What would you do? How could you pass away your time if you had no work to do? Men who retire at your age are always sorry: They wither away and die of dry rot."

"There'll be plenty for me to be doing," I told them. "I'll not be idle."

But still they argued. I was not greatly moved. They were thinking of me, and their arguments appealed to my selfish interests and needs, and just then I was not thinking very much about myself.

And then another sort of argument came to me. People wrote to me, men and women, who, like me, had lost their sons. Their letters brought the tears to my eyes anew. They were tender letters, and beautiful letters, most of them, and letters to make proud and glad, as well as sad, the heart of the man to whom they were written. I will not copy those letters down here, for they were written for my eyes, and for no others. But I can tell you the message that they all bore.

"Don't desert us now, Harry!" It was so that they put it, one after another, in those letters. "Ah, Harry – there is so much woe and grief and pain in the world that you, who can, must do all that is in your power to make them easier to bear! There are few forces enough in the world to-day to make us happy, even for a little space. Come back to us, Harry – make us laugh again!"

It was when those letters came that, for the first time, I saw that I had others to consider beside myself, and that it was not only my own wishes that I might take into account. I talked to my wife, and I told her of those letters, and there were tears in both our eyes as we thought about those folks who knew the sorrow that was in our hearts.

"You must think about them, Harry," she said.

And so I did think about them. And then I began to find that there were others still about whom I must think. There were three hundred people in the cast of "Three Cheers," at the Shaftesbury Theatre, in London. And I began to hear now that unless I went back the show would be closed, and all of them would be out of work. At that season of the year, in the theatrical world, it would be hard for them to find other engagements, and they were not, most of them, like me, able to live without the salaries from the show. They wrote to me, many of them, and begged me to come back. And I knew that it was a desperate time for anyone to be without employment. I had to think about those poor souls. And I could not bear the thought that I might be the means, however innocent, of bringing hardship and suffering upon others. It might not be my fault, and yet it would lie always upon my conscience.

Yet, even with all such thoughts and prayers to move me, I did not see how I could yield to them and go back. Even after I had come to the point of being willing to go back if I could, I did not think I could go through with it. I was afraid I would break down if I tried to play my part. I talked to Tom Vallance, my brother-in-law.

"It's very well to talk, Tom," I said. "But they'd ring the curtain down on me! I can never do it!"

"You must!" he said. "Harry, you must go back! It's your duty! What would the boy be saying and having you do? Don't you remember, Harry? John's last words to his men were – 'Carry On!' That's what it is they're asking you to do, too, Harry, and it's what John would have wanted. It would be his wish."

And I knew that he was right. Tom had found the one argument that could really move me and make me see my duty as the others did. So I gave in. I wired to the management that I would rejoin the cast of "Three Cheers," and I took the train to London. And as I rode in the train it seemed to me that the roar of the wheels made a refrain, and I could hear them pounding out those two words, in my boy's voice: "Carry On!"

But how hard it was to face the thought of going before an audience again! And especially in such circumstances. There were to be gayety and life and light and sparkle all about me. There were to be lassies, in their gay dresses, and the merriest music in London. And my part was to be merry, too, and to make the great audience laugh that I would see beyond the footlights. And I thought of the Merryman in The Yeomen of the Guard, and that I must be a little like him, though my cause for grief was different.

But I had given my word, and though I longed, again and again, as I rode toward London, and as the time drew near for my performance, to back out, there was no way that I could do so. And Tom Vallance did his best to cheer me and hearten me, and relieve my nervousness. I have never been so nervous before. Not since I made my first appearance before an audience have I been so near to stage fright.

I would not see anyone that night, when I reached the theatre. I stayed in my dressing-room, and Tom Vallance stayed with me, and kept everyone who tried to speak with me away. There were good folk, and kindly folk, friends of mine in the company, who wanted to shake my hand and tell me how they felt for me, but he knew that it was better for them not to see me yet, and he was my bodyguard.

"It's no use, Tom," I said to him, again and again, after I was dressed and in my make up. I was cold first, and then hot. And I trembled in every limb. "They'll have to ring the curtain down on me."

"You'll be all right, Harry," he said. "So soon as you're out there! Remember, they're all your friends!"

But he could not comfort me. I felt sure that it was a foolish thing for me to try to do; that I could not go through with it. And I was sorry, for the thousandth time, that I had let them persuade me to make the effort.

A call boy came at last to warn me that it was nearly time for my first entrance. I went with Tom into the wings, and stood there, waiting. I was pale under my make up, and I was shaking and trembling like a baby. And even then I wanted to cry off. But I remembered my boy, and those last words of his – "Carry On!" I must not fail him without at least trying to do what he would have wanted me to do!

My entrance was with a lilting little song called "I Love My Jean." And I knew that in a moment my cue would be given, and I would hear the music of that song beginning. I was as cold as if I had been in an icy street, although it was hot. I thought of the two thousand people who were waiting for me beyond the footlights – the house was a big one, and it was packed full that night.

"I can't, Tom – I can't!" I cried.

But he only smiled, and gave me a little push as my cue came and the music began. I could scarcely hear it; it was like music a great distance off, coming very faintly to my ears. And I said a prayer, inside. I asked God to be good to me once more, and to give me strength, and to bear me through this ordeal that I was facing, as he had borne me through before. And then I had to step into the full glare of the great lights.

I felt as if I were in a dream. The people were unreal – stretching away from me in long, sloping rows, their white faces staring at me from the darkness beyond the great lights. And there was a little ripple that ran through them as I went out, as if a great many people, all at the same moment, had caught their breath.

I stood and faced them, and the music sounded in my ears. For just a moment they were still. And then they were shaken by a mighty roar. They cheered and cheered and cheered. They stood up and waved to me. I could hear their voices rising, and cries coming to me, with my own name among them.

"Bravo, Harry!" I heard them call. And then there were more cheers, and a great clapping of hands. And I have been told that everywhere in that great audience men and women were crying, and that the tears were rolling down their cheeks without ever an attempt by any of them to hide them or to check them. It was the most wonderful and the most beautiful demonstration I have ever seen, in all the years that I have been upon the stage. Many and many a time audiences have been good to me. They have clapped me and they have cheered me, but never has an audience treated me as that one did. I had to use every bit of strength and courage that I had to keep from breaking down.

To this day I do not know how I got through with that first song that night. I do not even know whether I really sang it. But I think that, somehow, blindly, without knowing what I was doing, I did get through; I did sing it to the end. Habit, the way that I was used to it, I suppose, helped me to carry on. And when I left the stage the whole company, it seemed to me, was waiting for me. They were crying and laughing, hysterically, and they crowded around me, and kissed me, and hugged me, and wrung my hand.

It seemed that the worst of my ordeal was over. But in the last act I had to face another test.

There was a song for me in that last act that was the great song in London that season. I have sung it all over America since then "The Laddies Who Fought and Won." It has been successful everywhere – that song has been one of the most popular I have ever sung. But it was a cruel song for me to sing that night!

It was the climax of the last act and of the whole piece. In "Three Cheers" soldiers were brought on each night to be on the stage behind me when I sang that song. They were from the battalion of the Scots Guards in London, and they were real soldiers, in uniform. Different men were used each night, and the money that was paid to the Tommies for their work went into the company fund of the men who appeared, and helped to provide them with comforts and luxuries. And the war office was glad of the arrangement, too, for it was a great song to stimulate recruiting.

There were two lines in the refrain that I shall never forget. And it was when I came to those two lines that night that I did, indeed, break down. Here they are:

"When we all gather round the old fireside
And the fond mother kisses her son – "

Were they not cruel words for me to have to sing, who knew that his mother could never kiss my son again? They brought it all back to me! My son was gone – he would never come back with the laddies who had fought and won!

For a moment I could not go on. I was choking. The tears were in my eyes, and my throat was choked with sobs. But the music went on, and the chorus took up the song, and between the singers and the orchestra they covered the break my emotion had made. And in a little space I was able to go on with the next verse, and to carry on until my part in the show was done for the night. But I still wondered how it was that they had not had to ring down the curtain upon me, and that Tom Vallance and the others had been right and I the one that was wrong!

Ah, weel, I learned that night what many and many another Briton had learned, both at home and in France – that you can never know what you can do until you have to find it out! Yon was the hardest task ever I had to undertake, but for my boy's sake, and because they had made me understand that it was what he would have wanted me to do, I got through with it.

They rose to me again, and cheered and cheered, after I had finished singing "The Laddies Who Fought and Won." And there were those who called to me for a speech, but so much I had to deny them, good though they had been to me, and much as I loved them for the way they had received me. I had no words that night to thank them, and I could not have spoken from that stage had my life depended upon it. I could only get through, after my poor fashion, with my part in the show.

But the next night I did pull myself together, and I was able to say a few words to the audience – thanks that were simply and badly put, it may be, but that came from the bottom of my overflowing heart.

CHAPTER X

I had not believed it possible. But there I was, not only back at work, back upon the stage to which I thought I had said good-by forever, but successful as I had thought I could never be again. And so I decided that I would remain until the engagement of "Three Cheers" closed. But my mind was made up to retire after that engagement. I felt that I had done all I could, and that it was time for me to retire, and to cease trying to make others laugh. There was no laughter in my heart, and often and often, that season, as I cracked my merriest jokes, my heart was sore and heavy and the tears were in my eyes.

But slowly a new sort of courage came to me. I was able to meet my friends again, and to talk to them, of myself and of my boy. I met brother officers of his, and I heard tales of him that gave me a new and even greater pride in him than I had known before. And my friends begged me to carry on in every way.

"You were doing a great work and a good work, Harry," they said. "The boy would want you to carry on. Do not drop all the good you were doing."

I knew that they were right. To sit alone and give way to my grief was a selfish thing to do at such a time. If there was work for me to do, still, it was my duty to try to do it, no matter how greatly I would have preferred to rest quiet. At this time there was great need of making the people of Britain understand the need of food conservation, and so I began to go about London, making speeches on that subject wherever people could be gathered together to listen to me. They told me I did some good. And at least, I tried.

And before long I was glad, indeed, that I had listened to the counsel of my friends and had not given way to my selfish desire to nurse my grief in solitude and silence. For I realized that there was a real work for me to do. Those folk who had begged me to do my part in lightening the gloom of Britain had been right. There was so much sorrow and grief in the land that it was the duty of all who could dispel it, if even for a little space, to do what they could. I remembered that poem of Ella Wheeler Wilcox – "Laugh and the World Laughs With You!" And so I tried to laugh, and to make the part of the world that I chanced to be in laugh with me. For I knew there was weeping and sorrowing enough.

And all the time I felt that the spirit of my boy was with me, and that he knew what I was doing, and why, and was glad, and that he understood that if I laughed it was not because I thought less often of him, or missed him less keenly and bitterly than I had done from the very beginning.

There was much praise for my work from high officials, and it made me proud and glad to know that the men who were at the head of Britain's effort in the war thought I was being of use. One time I spoke with Mr. Balfour, the former Prime Minister, at Drury Lane Theatre to one of the greatest war gatherings that was ever held in London.

And always and everywhere there were the hospitals, full of the laddies who had been brought home from France. Ah, but they were pitiful, those laddies who had fought, and won, and been brought back to be nursed back to the life they had been so bravely willing to lay down for their country! But it was hard to look at them, and know how they were suffering, and to go through with the task I had set myself of cheering them and comforting them in my own way! There were times when it was all I could do to get through with my program.

They never complained. They were always bright and cheerful, no matter how terrible their wounds might be; no matter what sacrifices they had made of eyes and limbs. There were men in those hospitals who knew that they were going out no more than half the men they had been. And yet they were as brave and careless of themselves as if their wounds had been but trifles. I think the greatest exhibition of courage and nerve the world has ever seen was to be found in those hospitals in London and, indeed, all over Britain, where those wonderful lads kept up their spirits always, though they knew they could never again be sound in body.

Many and many of them there were who knew that they could never walk again the shady lanes of their hameland or the little streets of their hame towns! Many and many more there were who knew that, even after the bandages were taken from about their eyes, they would never gaze again upon the trees and the grass and the flowers growing upon their native hillsides; that never again could they look upon the faces of their loved ones. They knew that everlasting darkness was their portion upon this earth.

But one and all they talked and laughed and sang! And it was there among the hospitals, that I came to find true courage and good cheer. It was not there that I found talk of discouragement, and longing for any early peace, even though the final victory that could alone bring a real peace and a worthy peace had not been won. No – not in the hospitals could I find and hear such talk as that! For that I had to listen to those who had not gone – who had not had the courage and the nerve to offer all they had and all they were and go through that hell of hells that is modern war!

I saw other hospitals besides the ones in London. After a time, when I was very tired, and far from well, I went to Scotland for a space to build myself up and get some rest. And in the far north I went fishing on the River Dee, which runs through the Durrie estate. And while I was there the Laird heard of it. And he sent word to tell me of a tiny hospital hard by where a guid lady named Mrs. Baird was helping to nurse disabled men back to health and strength. He asked me would I no call upon the men and try to give them a little cheer. And I was glad to hear of the chance to help.

I laid down my rod forthwith, for here was better work than fishing – and in my ain country. They told me the way that I should go, and that this Mrs. Baird had turned a little school house into a convalescent home, and was doing a fine and wonderful work for the laddies she had taken in. So I set out to find it, and I walked along a country road to come to it.

Soon I saw a man, strong and hale, as it seemed, pushing a wheel chair along the road toward me. And in the chair sat a man, and I could see at once that he had lost the use of his legs – that he was paralyzed from the waist down. It was the way he called to him who was pushing him that made me tak notice.

"Go to the right, mon!" he would call. Or, a moment later, "To the left now."

And then they came near to the disaster. The one who was pushing was heading straight for the side of the road, and the one in the chair bellowed out to him:

"Whoa there!" he called. "Mon – ye're taking me into the ditch! Where would ye be going with me, anyway?"

And then I understood. The man who was pushing was blind! They had but the one pair of eyes and the one pair of legs between the two of them, and it was so that they contrived to go out together without taking help from anyone else! And they were both as cheerful as wee laddies out for a lark. It was great sport for them. And it was they who gave me my directions to get to Mrs. Baird's.

They disputed a little about the way. The blind man, puir laddie, thought he knew. And he did not – not quite. But he corrected the man who could see but could not walk.

"It's the wrong road you're giving the gentleman," he said. "It's the second turn he should be taking, not the first."

And the other would not argue with him. It was a kindly thing, the way he kept quiet, and did but wink at me, that I might know the truth. He trusted me to understand and to know why he was acting as he was, and I blessed him in my heart for his thoughtfulness. And so I thanked them, and passed on, and reached Mrs. Baird's, and found a royal welcome there, and when they asked me if I would sing for the soldiers, and I said it was for that that I had come, there were tears in Mrs. Baird's eyes. And so I gave a wee concert there, and sang my songs, and did my best to cheer up those boys.

Ah, my puir, brave Scotland – my bonnie little Scotland!

No part of all the United Kingdom, and, for that matter, no part of the world, has played a greater part, in proportion to its size and its ability, than has Scotland in this war for humanity against the black force that has attacked it. Nearly a million men has Scotland sent to the army – out of a total population of five million! One in five of all her people have gone. No country in the world has ever matched that record. Ah, there were no slackers in Scotland! And they are still going – they are still going! As fast as they are old enough, as fast as restrictions are removed, so that men are taken who were turned back at first by the recruiting officers, as fast as men see to it that some provision is made for those they must leave behind them, they are putting on the King's uniform and going out against the Hun. My country, my ain Scotland, is not great in area. It is not a rich country in worldly goods or money. But it is big with a bigness beyond measurement, it is rich beyond the wildest dreams of avarice, in patriotism, in love of country, and in bravery.

We have few young men left in Scotland. It is rarely indeed that in a Scottish village, in a glen, even in a city, you see a young man in these days. Only the very old are left, and the men of middle age. And you know why the young men you see are there. They cannot go, because, although their spirit is willing their flesh is too weak to let them go, for one reason or another. Factory and field and forge – all have been stripped to fill the Scottish regiments and keep them at their full strength. And in Scotland, as in England, women have stepped in to fill the places their men have left vacant. This war is not to be fought by men alone. Women have their part to play, and they are playing it nobly, day after day. The women of Scotland have seen their duty; they have heard their country's call, and they have answered it.

You will find it hard to discover anyone in domestic service to-day in Scotland. The folk who used to keep servants sent them packing long since, to work where they would be of more use to their country. The women of each household are doing the work about the house, little though they may have been accustomed to such tasks in the days of peace. And they glory and take pride in the knowledge that they are helping to fill a place in the munitions factories or in some other necessary war work.

Do not look along the Scottish roads for folk riding in motor cars for pleasure. Indeed, you will waste your time if you look for pleasure-making of any sort in

Scotland to-day. Scotland has gone back to her ancient business of war, and she is carrying it on in the most businesslike way, sternly and relentlessly. But that is true all over the United Kingdom; I do not claim that Scotland takes the war more seriously than the rest of Britain. But I do think that she has set an example by the way she has flung herself, tooth and nail, into the mighty task that confronts us all – all of us allies who are leagued against the Hun and his plan to conquer the world and make it bow its neck in submission under his iron heel.

Let me tell you how Scotland takes this war. Let me show you the homecoming of a Scottish soldier, back from the trenches on leave. Why, he is received with no more ceremony than if he were coming home from his day's work!

Donald – or Jock might be his name, or Andy! – steps from the train at his old hame town. He is fresh from the mud of the Flanders trenches, and all his possessions and his kit are on his back, so that he is more like a beast of burden than the natty creature old tradition taught us to think a soldier must always be. On his boots there are still dried blobs of mud from some hole in France that is like a crater in hell. His uniform will be pretty sure to be dirty, too, and torn, and perhaps, if you looked closely at it, you would see stains upon it that you might not be far wrong in guessing to be blood.

Leave long enough to let him come home to Scotland – a long road it is from France to Scotland these days! – has been a rare thing for Jock. He will have been campaigning a long time to earn it – months certainly, and maybe even years. Perhaps he was one of these who went out first. He may have been mentioned in dispatches: there may be a distinguished conduct medal hidden about him somewhere – worth all the iron crosses the Kaiser ever gave! He has seen many a bloody field, be sure of that. He has heard the sounding of the gas alarm, and maybe got a whiff of the dirty poison gas the Huns turned loose against our boys. He has looked Death in the face so often that he has grown used to him. But now he is back in Scotland, safe and sound, free from battle and the work of the trenches for a space, home to gain new strength for his next bout with Fritz across the water.

When he gets off the train Jock looks about him, from force of habit. But no one has come to the station to meet him, and he looks as if that gave him neither surprise nor concern. For a minute, perhaps, he will look around him, wondering, I think, that things are so much as they were, fixing in his mind the old familiar scenes that have brought him cheer so often in black, deadly nights in the trenches or in lonely billets out there in France. And then, quietly, and as if he were indeed just home from some short trip, he shifts his pack, so that it lies comfortably across his back, and trudges off. There would be cabs around the station, but it would not come into Jock's mind to hail one of the drivers. He has been used to using Shank's Mare in France when he wanted to go anywhere, and so now he sets off quietly, with his long, swinging soldier's stride.

As he walks along he is among scenes familiar to him since his boyhood. Yon house, yon barn, yon wooded rise against the sky are landmarks for him. And he is pretty sure to meet old friends. They nod to him, pleasantly, and with a smile, but there is no excitement, no strangeness, in their greeting. For all the emotion they show, these folk to whom he has come back, as from the grave, they might have seen him yesterday, and the day before that, and the war never have been at all. And Jock thinks nothing of it that they are not more excited about him. You and I may be thinking of Jock as a hero, but that is not his idea about himself. He is just a Tommy, home on leave from France – one of a hundred thousand, maybe. And if he thought at all about the way his home folk greeted him it would be just so – that he could not expect them to be making a fuss about one soldier out of so many. And, since he, Jock, is not much excited, not much worked up, because he is seeing these good folk again, he does not think it strange that they are not more excited about the sight of him. It would be if they did make a fuss over him, and welcome him loudly, that he would think it strange!

And at last he comes to his own old home. He will stop and look around a bit. Maybe he has seen that old house a thousand times out there, tried to remember every line and corner of it. And maybe, as he looks down the quiet village street, he is thinking of how different France was. And, deep down in his heart, Jock is glad that everything is as it was, and that nothing has been changed. He could not tell you why; he could not put his feeling into words. But it is there, deep down, and the truer and the keener because it is so deep. Ah, Jock may take it quietly, and there may be no way for him to show his heart, but he is glad to be home!

And at his gate will come, as a rule, Jock's first real greeting. A dog, grown old since his departure, will come out, wagging his tail, and licking the soldier's hand. And Jock will lean down, and give his old dog a pat. If the dog had not come he would have been surprised and disappointed. And so, glad with every fibre of his being, Jock goes in, and finds father and mother and sisters within. They look up at his coming, and their happiness shines for a moment in their eyes. But they are not the sort of people to show their emotions or make a fuss. Mother and girls will rise and kiss him, and begin to take his gear, and his father will shake him by the hand.

"Well," the father will ask, "how are you getting along, lad?"

And – "All right," he will answer. That is the British soldier's answer to that question, always and everywhere.

Then he sits down, happy and at rest, and lights his pipe, maybe, and looks about the old room which holds so many memories for him. And supper will be ready, you may be sure. They will not have much to say, these folk of Jock's, but if you look at his face as dish after dish is set before him, you will understand that this is a feast that has been prepared for him. They may have been going without all sorts of good things themselves, but they have contrived, in some fashion, to have them all for Jock. All Scotland has tightened its belt, and done its part, in that fashion, as in every other, toward the winning of the war. But for the soldiers the best is none too good. And Jock's folk would rather make him welcome so, by proof that takes no words, than by demonstrations of delight and of affection.

As he eats, they gather round him at the board, and they tell him all the gossip of the neighborhood. He does not talk about the war, and, if they are curious – probably they are not! – they do not ask him questions. They think that he wants to forget about the war and the trenches and the mud, and they are right. And so, after he has eaten his fill, he lights his pipe again, and sits about. And maybe, as it grows dark, he takes a bit walk into town. He walks slowly, as if he is glad that for once he need not be in a hurry, and he stops to look into shop windows as if he had never seen their stocks before, though you may be sure that, in a Scottish village, he has seen everything they have to offer hundreds of times.

He will meet friends, maybe, and they will stop and nod to him. And perhaps one of six will stop longer.

"How are you getting on, Jock?" will be the question.

"All right!" Jock will say. And he will think the question rather fatuous, maybe. If he were not all right, how should he be there? But if Jock had lost both legs, or an arm, or if he had been blinded, that would still be his answer. Those words have become a sort of slogan for the British army, that typify its spirit.

Jock's walk is soon over, and he goes home, by an old path that is known to him, every foot of it, and goes to bed in his own old bed. He has not broken into the routine of the household, and he sees no reason why he should. And the next day it is much the same for him. He gets up as early as he ever did, and he is likely to do a few odd bits of work that his father has not had time to come to. He talks with his mother and the girls of all sorts of little, commonplace things, and with his father he discusses the affairs of the community. And in the evening he strolls down town again, and exchanges a few words with friends, and learns, perhaps, of boys who haven't been lucky enough to get home on leave – of boys with whom he grew up, who have gone west.

So it goes on for several days, each day the same. Jock is quietly happy. It is no task to entertain him: he does not want to be entertained. The peace and quiet of home are enough for him; they are change enough from the turmoil of the front and the ceaseless grind of the life in the army in France.

And then Jock's leave nears its end, and it is time for him to go back. He tells them, and he makes his few small preparations. They will have cleaned his kit for him, and mended some of his things that needed mending. And when it is time for him to go they help him on with his pack and he kisses his mother and the girls good-by, and shakes hands with his father.

"Well, good-by," Jock says. He might be going to work in a factory a few miles off. "I'll be all right. Good-by, now. Don't you cry, now, mother, and you, Jeannie and Maggie. Don't you fash yourselves about me. I'll be back again. And if I shouldn't come back – why, I'll be all right."

So he goes, and they stand looking after him, and his old dog wonders why he is going, and where, and makes a move to follow him, maybe. But he marches off down the street, alone, never looking back, and is waiting when the train comes. It will be full of other Jocks and Andrews and Tams, on their way back to France, like him, and he will nod to some he knows as he settles down in the carriage.

And in just two days Jock will have traveled the length of England, and crossed the channel, and ridden up to the front. He will have reported himself, and have been ordered, with his company, into the trenches. And on the third night, had you followed him, you might see him peering over the parapet at the lines of the Hun, across No Man's Land, and listening to the whine of bullets and the shriek of shells over his head, with a star shell, maybe, to throw a green light upon him for a moment.

So it is that a warrior comes and that a warrior goes in a land where war is war; in a land where war has become the business of all every day, and has settled down into a matter of routine.

CHAPTER XI

I could not, much as I should in many ways have liked to do so, prolong my stay in Scotland. The peace and the restfulness of the Highlands, the charm of the heather and the hills, the long, lazy days with my rod, whipping some favorite stream – ah, they made me happy for a moment, but they could not make me forget! My duty called me back, and the thought of war, and suffering, and there were moments when it seemed to me that nothing could keep me from plunging again into the work I had set out to do.

In those days I was far too restless to be taking my ease at home, in my wee hoose at Dunoon. A thousand activities called me. The rest had been necessary; I had had to admit that, and to obey my doctor, for I had been feeling the strain of my long continued activity, piled up, as it was, on top of my grief and care. And yet I was eager to be off and about my work again.

I did not want to go back to the same work I had been doing. No! I was still a young man. I was younger than men and officers who were taking their turn in the trenches. I was but forty-six years old, and there was a lot of life and snap in the old dog yet! My life had been rightly lived. As a young man I had worked in a pit, ye ken, and that had given me a strength in my back and my legs that would have served me well in the trenches. War, these days, means hard work as well as fighting – more, indeed. War is a business, a great industry, now. There is all manner of work that must be done at the front and right behind it. Aye, and I was eager to be there and to be doing my share of it – and not for the first time.

Many a time, and often, I had broached my idea of being allowed to enlist, e'en before the Huns killed my boy. But they would no listen to me. They told me, each time, that there was more and better work for me to do at hame in Britain, spurring others on, cheering them when they came back maimed and broken, getting the country to put its shoulder to the wheel when it came to subscribing to the war loans and all the rest of it. And it seemed to me that it was not for me to decide; that I must obey those who were better in a position to judge than I could be.

I went down south to England, and I talked again of enlisting and trying to get a crack at those who had killed my boy. And again my friends refused to listen to me.

"Why, Harry," they said to me – and not my own friends, only, but men highly placed enough to make me know that I must pay heed to what they said – "you must not think of it! If you enlisted, or if we got you a commission, you'd be but one man out there. Here you're worth many men – a brigade, or a division, maybe. You are more use to us than many men who go out there to fight. You do great things toward winning the war every day. No, Harry, there is work for every man in Britain to do, and you have found yours and are doing it."

I was not content, though, even when I seemed to agree with them. I did try to argue, but it was no use. And still I felt that it was no time for a man to be playing and to be giving so much of his time to making others gay. It was well for folk to laugh, and to get their minds off the horror of war for a little time. Well I knew! Aye, and I believed that I was doing good, some good at least, and giving cheer to some puir laddies who needed it sorely. But – weel, it was no what I wanted to be doing when my country was fighting for her life! I made up my mind, slowly, what it was that I wanted to do that would fit in with the ideas and wishes of those whose word I was bound to heed and that would still come closer than what I was doing to meet my own desires.

Every day, nearly, then, I was getting letters from the front. They came from laddies whom I'd helped to make up their minds that they belonged over yon, where the men were. Some were from boys who came from aboot Dunoon. I'd known those laddies since they were bits o' bairns, most of them. And then there were letters – and they touched me as much and came as close home as any of them – from boys who were utter strangers to me, but who told me they felt they knew me because they'd seen me on the stage, or because their phonograph, maybe, played some of my records, and because they'd read that my boy had shared their dangers and given his life, as they were ready, one and all, to do.

And those letters, nearly all, had the same refrain. They wanted me. They wanted me to come to them, since they couldn't be coming to me.

"Come on out here and see us and sing for us, Harry," they'd write to me. "It'd be a fair treat to see your mug and hear you singing about the wee hoose amang the heather or the bonnie, bonnie lassie!"

How could a man get such a plea as that and not want to do what those laddies asked? How could he think of the great deal they were doing and not want to do the little bit they asked of him? But it was no a simple matter, ye'll ken! I could not pack a bag and start for France from Charing Cross or Victoria as I might have done – and often did – before the war. No one might go to France unless he had passports and leave from the war office, and many another sort of arrangement there was to make. But I set wheels in motion.

Just to go to France to sing for the boys would have been easy enough. They told me that at once.

"What? Harry Lauder wants to go to France to sing for the soldiers? He shall – whenever he pleases! Tell him we'll be glad to send him!"

So said the war office. But I knew what they meant. They meant for me to go to one or more of the British bases and give concerts. There were troops moving in and out of the bases all the time; men who'd been in the trenches or in action in an offensive and were back in rest billets, or even further back, were there in their thousands. But it was the real front I was eager to reach. I wanted to be where my boy had been, and to see his grave. I wanted to sing for the laddies who were bearing the brunt of the big job over there – while they were bearing it.

And that no one had done. Many of our leading actors and singers and other entertainers were going back and forth to France all the time. Never a week went by but they were helping to cheer up the boys at the bases. It was a grand work they were doing, and the boys were grateful to them, and all Britain should share that gratitude. But it was a wee bit more that I wanted to be doing, and there was the rub.

I wanted to go up to the battle lines themselves and to sing for the boys who were in the thick of the struggle with the Hun. I wanted to give a concert in a front-line trench where the Huns could hear me, if they cared to listen. I wanted them to learn once more the lesson we could never teach them often enough – the lesson of the spirit of the British army, that could go into battle with a laugh on its lips.

But at first I got no encouragement at all when I told what it was in my mind to do. My friends who had influence shook their heads.

"I'm afraid it can't be managed, Harry," they told me. "It's never been done."

I told them what I believed myself, and what I have often thought of when things looked hard and prospects were dark. I told them everything had to be done for the first time sometime, and I begged them not to give up the effort to win my way for me. And so I knew that when they told me no one had done it before it wasn't reason enough why I shouldn't do it. And I made up my mind that I would be the pioneer in giving concerts under fire if that should turn out to be a part of the contract.

But I could not argue. I could only say what it was that I wanted to do, and wait the pleasure of those whose duty it was to decide. I couldn't tell the military authorities where they must send me. It was for me to obey when they gave their orders, and to go wherever they thought I would do the most good. I would not have you thinking that I was naming conditions, and saying I would go where I pleased or bide at hame! That was not my way. All I could do was to hope that in the end they would see matters as I did and so decide to let me have my way. But I was ready for my orders, whatever they might be.

There was one thing I wanted, above all others, to do when I got to France, and so much I said. I wanted to meet the Highland Brigade, and see the bonnie laddies in their kilts as the Huns saw them – the Huns, who called them the Ladies from Hell, and hated them worse than they hated any troops in the whole British army.

Ha' ye heard the tale of the Scotsman and the Jew? Sandy and Ikey they were, and they were having a disputatious argument together. Each said he could name more great men of his race who were famous in history than the other could. And they argued, and nearly came to blows, and were no further along until they thought of making a bet. An odd bet it was. For each great name that Sandy named of a Scot whom history had honored he was to pull out one of Ikey's hairs, and Ikey was to have the same privilege.

"Do ye begin!" said Sandy.

"Moses!" said Ikey, and pulled.

"Bobbie Burns!" cried Sandy, and returned the compliment.

"Abraham!" said Ikey, and pulled again.

"Ouch – Duggie Haig!" said Sandy.

And then Ikey grabbed a handful of hairs at once.

"Joseph and his brethren!" he said, gloating a bit as he watched the tears starting from Sandy's eyes at the pain of losing so many good hairs at once.

"So it's pulling them out in bunches ye are!" said Sandy. "Ah, well, man –" And he reached with both his hands for Ikey's thatch.

"The Hieland Brigade!" he roared, and pulled all the hairs his two hands would hold!

Ah, weel, there are sad thoughts that come to me, as well as proud and happy ones, when I think of the bonnie kilted laddies who fought and died so nobly out there against the Hun! They were my own laddies, those, and it was with them and amang them that my boy went to his death. It was amang them I would find, I thought, those who could tell me more than I knew of how he had died, and of how he had lived before he died. And I thought the boys of the brigade would be glad to see me and to hear my songs – songs of their hames and their ain land, auld Scotland. And so I used what influence I had, and did not think it wrong to employ at such a time, and in such a cause. For I knew that if they sent me to the Hieland Brigade they would be sending me to the front of the front line – for that was where I would have to go seeking the Hieland laddies!

I waited as patiently as I could. And then one day I got my orders! I was delighted, for the thing they had told me could not be done had actually been arranged for me. I was asked to get ready to go to France to entertain the soldiers, and it was the happiest day I had known since I had heard of my boy's death.

There was not much for me to do in the way of making ready. The whole trip, of course, would be a military one. I might be setting out as a minstrel for France, but every detail of my arrangements had to be made in accordance with military rules, and once I reached France I would be under the orders of the army in every movement I might make. All that was carefully explained to me.

But still there were things for me to think about and to arrange. I wanted some sort of accompaniment for my songs, and how to get it puzzled me for a time. But there was a firm in London that made pianos that heard of my coming trip, and solved that problem for me. They built, and they presented to me, the weest piano ever you saw – a piano so wee that it could be carried in an ordinary motor car. Only five octaves it had, but it was big enough, and sma' enough at once. I was delighted with it, and so were all who saw it. It weighed only about a hundred and fifty pounds – less than even a middling stout man! And it was cunningly built, so that no space at all was wasted. Mrs. Lauder, when she saw it, called it cute, and so did every other woman who laid eyes upon it. It was designed to be carried on the grid of a motor car – and so it was, for many miles of shell-torn roads!

When I was sure of my piano I thought of another thing it would be well for me to take with me. And so I spent a hundred pounds – five hundred American dollars – for cigarettes. I knew they would be welcome everywhere I went. It makes no matter how many cigarettes we send to France, there will never be enough.

My friends thought I was making a mistake in taking so many; they were afraid they would make matters hard when it came to transportation, and reminded me that I faced difficulties in that respect in France it was nearly impossible for us at home in Britain to visualize at all. But I had my mind and my heart set on getting those fags – a cigarette is a fag to every British soldier – to my destination with me. Indeed, I thought they would mean more to the laddies out there than I could hope to do myself!

I was not to travel alone. My tour was to include two traveling companions of distinction and fame. One was James Hogge, M.P., member from East Edinburgh, who was eager, as so many members of Parliament were, to see for himself how things were at the front. James Hogge was one of the members most liked by the soldiers. He had worked hard for them, and gained – and well earned – much fame by the way he struggled with the matter of getting the right sort of pensions for the laddies who were offering their lives.

The other distinguished companion I was to have was an old and good friend of mine, the Reverend George Adam, then a secretary to the Minister of Munitions. He lived in Ilford, a suburb of London, then, but is now in Montreal, Canada. I was glad of the opportunity to travel with both these men, for I knew that one's traveling companions, on such a tour, were of the utmost importance in determining its success or failure, and I could not have chosen a better pair, had the choice been left to me – which, of course, it was not.

There we were, you see – the Reverend George Adam, Harry Lauder and James Hogge, M.P. And no sooner did the soldiers hear of the combination than our tour was named "The Reverend Harry Lauder, M.P., Tour" was what we were called! And that absurd name stuck to us through our whole journey, in France, up and down the battle line, and until we came home to England and broke up!

CHAPTER XII

Up to that time I had thought I knew a good deal about the war. I had had much news from my boy. I had talked, I think, to as many returned soldiers as any man in Britain. I had seen much of the backwash and the wretched aftermath of war. Ah, yes, I thought I knew more than most folk did of what war meant! But until my tour began, as I see now, easily enough, I knew nothing – literally nothing at all!

There are towns and ports in Britain that are military areas. One may not enter them except upon business, the urgency of which has been established to the satisfaction of the military authorities. One must have a permit to live in them, even if they be one's home town. These towns are vital to the war and its successful prosecution.

Until one has seen a British port of embarkation in this war one has no real beginning, even, of a conception of the task the war has imposed upon Britain. It was so with me, I know, and since then other men have told me the same thing. There the army begins to pour into the funnel, so to speak, that leads to France and the front. There all sorts of lines are brought together, all sorts of scattered activities come to a focus. There is incessant activity, day and night.

It was from Folkestone, on the southeast coast, that the Reverend Harry Lauder, M.P. Tour was to embark. And we reached Folkestone on June 7, 1917.

Folkestone, in time of peace, was one of the greatest of the Southern watering places. It is a lovely spot. Great hotels line the Leas, a glorious promenade, along the top of chalk cliffs, that looks out over the Channel. In the distance one fancies one may see the coast of France, beyond the blue water.

There is green grass everywhere behind the beach. Folkestone has a miniature harbor, that in time of peace gave shelter to the fishing fleet and to the channel steamers that plied to and from Boulogne, in France. The harbor is guarded by stone jetties. It has been greatly enlarged now – so has all Folkestone, for that matter. But I am remembering the town as it was in peace!

There was no pleasanter and kindlier resort along that coast. The beach was wonderful, and all summer long it attracted bathers and children at play. Bathing machines lined the beach, of course, within the limits of the town; those queer, old, clumsy looking wagons, with a dressing cabin on wheels, that were drawn up and down according to the tide, so that bathers might enter the water from them directly. There, as in most British towns, women bathed at one part of the beach, men at the other, and all in the most decorous and modest of costumes.

But at Folkestone, in the old days of peace, about a mile from the town limits, there was another stretch of beach where all the gay folk bathed – men and women together. And there the costumes were such as might be seen at Deauville or Ostend, Etretat or Trouville. Highly they scandalized the good folk of Folkestone, to be sure – but little was said, and nothing was done, for, after all those were the folk who spent the money! They dressed in white tents that gleamed against the sea, and a pretty splash of color they made on a bright day for the soberer folk to go and watch, as they sat on the low chalk cliffs above them!

Gone – gone! Such days have passed for Folkestone! They will no doubt come again – but when? When?

June the seventh! Folkestone should have been gay for the beginning of the onset of summer visitors. Sea bathing should just have been beginning to be attractive, as the sun warmed the sea and the beach. But when we reached the town war was over all. Men in uniform were everywhere. Warships lay outside the harbor. Khaki and guns, men trudging along, bearing the burdens of war, motor trucks, rushing ponderously along, carrying ammunition and food, messengers on motorcycles, sounding to all traffic that might be in the way the clamorous summons to clear the path – those were the sights we saw!

How hopelessly confused it all seemed! I could not believe that there was order in the chaos that I saw. But that was because the key to all that bewildering activity was not in my possession.

Every man had his appointed task. He was a cog in the greatest machine the world has ever seen. He knew just what he was to do, and how much time had been allowed for the performance of his task. It was assumed he would not fail. The British army makes that assumption, and it is warranted.

I hear praise, even from men who hate the Hun as I hate him, for the superb military organization of the German army. They say the Kaiser's people may well take pride in that. But I say that I am prouder of what Britain and the new British army that has come into being since this war began have done than any German has a right to be! They spent forty-four years in making ready for a war they knew they meant, some day, to fight. We had not had, that day that I first saw our machine really functioning, as many months for preparation as they had had years. And yet we were doing our part.

We had had to build and prepare while we helped our ally, France, to hold off that gray horde that had swept down so treacherously through Belgium from the north and east. It was as if we had organized and trained and equipped a fire brigade while the fire was burning, and while our first devoted fighters sought to keep it in check with water buckets. And they did! They did! The water buckets served while the hose was made, and the mains were laid, and the hydrants set in place, and the trained firemen were made ready to take up the task.

And, now that I had come to Folkestone, now that I was seeing the results of all the labor that had been performed, the effect of all the prodigies of organization, I began to know what Lord Kitchener and those who had worked with him had done. System ruled everything at Folkestone. Nothing, it seemed to me, as officers explained as much as they properly could, had been left to chance. Here was order indeed.

In the air above us airplanes flew to and fro. They circled about like great, watchful hawks. They looped and whirled around, cutting this way and that, circling always. And I knew that, as they flew about outside the harbor the men in them were never off their guard; that they were peering down, watching every moment for the first trace of a submarine that might have crept through the more remote defenses of the Channel. Let a submarine appear – its shrift would be short indeed!

There, above, waited the airplanes. And on the surface of the sea sinister destroyers darted about as watchful as the flyers above, ready for any emergency that might arise. I have no doubt that submarines of our own lurked below, waiting, too, to do their part. But those, if any there were, I did not see. And one asks no questions at a place like Folkestone. I was glad of any information an officer might voluntarily give me. But it was not for me or any other loyal Briton to put him in the position of having to refuse to answer.

Soon a great transport was pointed out to me, lying beside the jetty. Gangplanks were down, and up them streams of men in khaki moved endlessly. Up they went, in an endless brown river, to disappear into the ship. The whole ship was a very hive of activity. Not only men were going aboard, but supplies of every sort; boxes of ammunition, stores, food. And I understood, and was presently to see, that beyond her sides there was the same ordered scene as prevailed on shore. Every man knew his task; the stowing away of everything that was being carried aboard was being carried out systematically and with the utmost possible economy of time and effort.

"That's the ship you will cross the Channel on," I was told. And I regarded her with a new interest. I do not know what part she had been wont to play in time of peace; what useful, pleasant journeys it had been her part to complete, I only knew that she was to carry me to France, and to the place where my heart was and for a long time had been. Me – and two thousand men who were to be of real use over there!

We were nearly the last to go on board. We found the decks swarming with men. Ah, the braw laddies! They smoked and they laughed as they settled themselves for the trip. Never a one looked as though he might be sorry to be there. They were leaving behind them all the good things, all the pleasant things, of life as, in time of peace, every one of them had learned to live it and to know it. Long, long since had the last illusion faded of the old days when war had seemed a thing of pomp and circumstance and glory.

They knew well, those boys, what it was they faced. Hard, grinding work they could look forward to doing; such work as few of them had ever known in the old days. Death and wounds they could reckon upon as the portion of just about so many of them. There would be bitter cold, later, in the trenches, and mud, and standing for hours in icy mud and water. There would be hard fare, and scanty, sometimes, when things went wrong. There would be gas attacks, and the bursting of shells about them with all sorts of poisons in them. Always there would be the deadliest perils of these perilous days.

But they sang as they set out upon the great adventure of their lives. They smiled and laughed. They cheered me, so that the tears started from my eyes, when they saw me, and they called the gayest of gay greetings, though they knew that I was going only for a little while, and that many of them had set foot on British soil for the last time. The steady babble of their voices came to our ears, and they swarmed below us like ants as they disposed themselves about the decks, and made the most of the scanty space that was allowed for them. The trip was to be short, of course; there were too few ships, and the problems of convoy were too great, to make it possible to make the voyage a comfortable one. It was a case of getting them over as might best be arranged.

A word of command rang out and was passed around by officers and non coms.

"Life belts must be put on before the ship sails!"

That simple order brought home the grim facts of war at that moment as scarcely anything else could have done. Here was a grim warning of the peril that lurked outside. Everywhere men were scurrying to obey – I among the rest. The order applied as much to us civilians as it did to any of the soldiers. And my belt did not fit, and was hard, extremely hard, for me to don. I could no manage it at all by myself, but Adam and Hogge had had an easier time with theirs, and they came to my help. Among us we got mine on, and Hogge stood off, and looked at me, and smiled.

"An extraordinary effect, Harry!" he said, with a smile. "I declare – it gives you the most charming embonpoint!"

I had my doubts about his use of the word charming. I know that I should not have cared to have anyone judge of my looks from a picture taken as I looked then, had one been taken.

But it was not a time for such thoughts. For a civilian, especially, and one not used to journeys in such times as these, there is a thrill and a solemnity about the donning of a life preserver. I felt that I was indeed, it might be, taking a risk in making this journey, and it was an awesome thought that I, too, might have seen my native land for the last time, and said a real good-by to those whom I had left behind me.

Now we cast off, and began to move, and a thrill ran through me such as I had never known before in all my life. I went to the rail as we turned our nose toward the open sea. A destroyer was ahead, another was beside us, others rode steadily along on either side. It was the most reassuring of sights to see them. They looked so business like, so capable. I could not imagine a Hun submarine as able to evade their watchfulness. And moreover, there were the watchful man birds above us, the circling airplanes, that could make out, so much better than could any lookout on a ship, the first trace of the presence of a tin fish. No – I was not afraid! I trusted in the British navy, which had guarded the sea lane so well that not a man had lost his life as the result of a Hun attack, although many millions had gone back and forth to France since the beginning of the war.

I did not stay with my own party. I preferred to move about among the Soldiers. I was deeply interested in them, as I have always been. And I wanted to make friends among them, and see how they felt.

"Lor' lumme – its old 'Arry Lauder!" said one cockney. "God bless you, 'Arry – many's the time I've sung with you in the 'alls. It's good to see you with us!"

And so I was greeted everywhere. Man after man crowded around me to shake hands. It brought a lump into my throat to be greeted so, and it made me more than ever glad that the military authorities had been able to see their way to grant my request. It confirmed my belief that I was going where I might be really useful to the men who were ready and willing to make the greatest of all sacrifices in the cause so close to all our hearts.

When I first went aboard the transport I picked up a little gold stripe. It was one of those men wear who have been wounded, as a badge of honor. I hoped I might be able to find the man who had lost it, and return it to him. But none of them claimed it, and I have kept it, to this day, as a souvenir of that voyage.

It was easy for them to know me. I wore my kilt and my cap, and my knife in my stocking, as I have always done, on the stage, and nearly always off it as well. And so they recognized me without difficulty. And never a one called me anything but Harry – except when it was 'Arry! I think I would be much affronted if ever a British soldier called me Mr. Lauder. I don't know – because not one of them ever did, and I hope none ever will!

They told me that there were men from the Highlands on board, and I went looking for them, and found them after a time, though going about that ship, so crowded she was, was no easy matter. They were Gordon Highlanders, mostly, I found, and they were glad to see me, and made me welcome, and I had a pipe with them, and a good talk.

Many of them were going back, after having been at home, recuperating from wounds. And they and the new men too were all eager and anxious to be put there and at work.

"Gie us a chance at the Huns – it's all we're asking," said one of a new draft. "They're telling us they don't like the sight of our kilts, Harry, and that a Hun's got less stomach for the cold steel of a bayonet than for anything else on earth. Weel – we're carrying a dose of it for them!"

And the men who had been out before, and were taking back with them the scars they had earned, were just as anxious as the rest. That was the spirit of every man on board. They did not like war as war, but they knew that this was a war that must be fought to the finish, and never a man of them wanted peace to come until Fritz had learned his lesson to the bottom of the last grim page.

I never heard a word of the danger of meeting a submarine. The idea that one might send a torpedo after us popped into my mind once or twice, but when it did I looked out at the destroyers, guarding us, and the airplanes above, and I felt as safe as if I had been in bed in my wee hoose at Dunoon. It was a true highway of war that those whippets of the sea had made the Channel crossing.

Ahm, but I was proud that day of the British navy! It is a great task that it has performed, and nobly it has done it. And it was proud and glad I was again when we sighted land, as we soon did, and I knew that I was gazing, for the first time since war had been declared, upon the shores of our great ally, France. It was the great day and the proud day and the happy day for me!

I was near the realizing of an old dream I had often had. I was with the soldiers who had my love and my devotion, and I was coming to France – the France that every Scotchman learns to love at his mother's breast.

A stir ran through the men. Orders began to fly, and I went back to my place and my party. Soon we would be ashore, and I would be in the way of beginning the work I had come to do.

CHAPTER XIII

Boulogne!

Like Folkestone, Boulogne, in happier times, had been a watering place, less fashionable than some on the French coast, but the pleasant resort of many in search of health and pleasure. And like Folkestone it had suffered the blight of war. The war had laid its heavy hand upon the port. It ruled everything; it was omnipresent. From the moment when we came into full view of the harbor it was impossible to think of anything else.

Folkestone had made me think of the mouth of a great funnel, into which all broad Britain had been pouring men and guns and all the manifold supplies and stores of modern war. And the trip across the narrow, well guarded lane in the Channel had been like the pouring of water through the neck of that same funnel. Here in Boulogne was the opening. Here the stream of men and supplies spread out to begin its orderly, irresistible flow to the front.

All of northern France and Belgium lay before that stream; it had to cover all the great length of the British front. Not from Boulogne alone, of course; I knew of Dunkirk and Calais, and guessed at other ports. There were other funnels, and into all of them, day after day, Britain was pouring her tribute; through all of them she was offering her sacrifice, to be laid upon the altar of strife.

Here, much more than at Folkestone, as it chanced, I saw at once another thing. There was a double funnel. The stream ran both ways. For, as we steamed into Boulogne, a ship was coming out – a ship with a grim and tragic burden. She was one of our hospital ships. But she was guarded as carefully by destroyers and aircraft as our transport had been. The Red Cross meant nothing to the Hun – except, perhaps, a shining target. Ship after ship that bore that symbol of mercy and of pain had been sunk. No longer did our navy dare to trust the Red Cross. It took every precaution it could take to protect the poor fellows who were going home to Blighty.

As we made our way slowly in, through the crowded harbor, full of transports, of ammunition ships, of food carriers, of destroyers and small naval craft of all sorts, I began to be able to see more and more of what was afoot ashore. It was near noon; the day that had been chosen for my arrival in France was one of brilliant sunshine and a cloudless sky. And my eyes were drawn to other hospital ships that were waiting at the docks. Motor ambulances came dashing up, one after the other, in what seemed to me to be an endless stream. The pity of that sight! It was as if I could peer through the intervening space and see the bandaged heads, the places where limbs had been, the steadfast gaze of the boys who were being carried up in stretchers. They had done their task, a great number of them; they had given all that God would let them give to King and country. Life was left to them, to be sure; most of these boys were sure to live.

But to what maimed and incomplete lives were they doomed! The thousands who would be cripples always – blind, some of them, and helpless, dependent upon what others might choose or be able to do for them. It was then, in that moment, that an idea was born, vaguely, in my mind, of which I shall have much more to say later.

There was beauty in that harbor of Boulogne. The sun gleamed against the chalk cliffs. It caught the wings of airplanes, flying high above us. But there was little of beauty in my mind's eye. That could see through the surface beauty of the scene and of the day to the grim, stark ugliness of war that lay beneath.

I saw the ordered piles of boxes and supplies, the bright guns, with the sun reflected from their barrels, dulled though these were to prevent that very thing. And I thought of the waste that was involved – of how all this vast product of industry was destined to be destroyed, as swiftly as might be, bringing no useful accomplishment with its destruction – save, of course, that accomplishment which must be completed before any useful thing may be done again in this world.

Then we went ashore, and I could scarcely believe that we were indeed in France, that land which, friends though our nations are, is at heart and in spirit so different from my own country. Boulogne had ceased to be French, indeed. The port was like a bit of Britain picked up, carried across the Channel and transplanted successfully to a new resting-place.

English was spoken everywhere – and much of it was the English of the cockney, innocent of the aitch, and redolent of that strange tongue. But it is no for me, a Scot, to speak of how any other man uses the King's English! Well I ken it! It was good to hear it – had there been a thought in my mind of being homesick, it would quickly have been dispelled. The streets rang to the tread of British soldiers; our uniform was everywhere. There were Frenchmen, too; they were attached, many of them, for one reason and another, to the British forces. But most of them spoke English too.

I had most care about the unloading of my cigarettes. It was a point of honor with me, by now, after the way my friends had joked me about them, to see that every last one of the "fags" I had brought with me reached a British Tommy. So to them I gave my first care. Then I saw to the unloading of my wee piano, and, having done so, was free to go with the other members of the Reverend Harry Lauder, M.P., Tour to the small hotel that was to be headquarters for all of us in Boulogne.

Arrangements had to be made for my debut in France, and I can tell you that no professional engagement I have ever filled ever gave me half so much concern as this one! I have sung before many strange audiences, in all parts of the world, or nearly all. I have sung for folk who had no idea of what to expect from me, and have known that I must be at work from the moment of my first appearance on the stage to win them. But these audiences that I was to face here in France gave me more thought than any of them. I had so great a reason for wanting to succeed with them!

And here, ye ken, I faced conditions that were harder than had ever fallen to my lot. I was not to have, most of the time, even the military theaters that had, in some cases, been built for the men behind the lines, where many actors and, indeed, whole companies, from home had been appearing. I could make no changes of costume. I would have no orchestra. Part of the time I would have my wee piano, but I reckoned on going to places where even that sma' thing could no follow me.

But I had a good manager – the British army, no less! It was the army that had arranged my booking. We were not left alone, not for a minute. I would not have you think that we were left to go around on our own, and as we pleased. Far from it! No sooner had we landed than Captain Roberts, D.S.O., told me, in a brief, soldierly way, that was also extremely businesslike, what sort of plans had been made for us.

"We have a number of big hospitals here," he said. "This is one of the important British bases, as you know, and it is one of those where many of our men are treated before they are sent home. So, since you are here, we thought you would want to give your first concerts to the wounded men here."

So I learned that the opening of what you might call my engagement in the trenches was to be in hospitals. That was not new to me, and yet I was to find that there was a difference between a base hospital in France and the sort of hospitals I had seen so often at home.

Nothing, indeed, was left to us. After Captain Roberts had explained matters, we met Captain Godfrey, who was to travel with us, and be our guide, our military mentor and our ruler. We understood that we must place ourselves under him, and under military discipline. No Tommy, indeed, was more under discipline than we had to be. But we did not chafe, civilians though we were. When you see the British army at work nothing is further from your thoughts than to criticize or to offer any suggestions. It knows its business, and does it, quietly and without fuss. But even Fritz has learned to be chary of getting in the way when the British army has made up its mind – and that is what he is there for, though I've no doubt that Fritz himself would give a pretty penny to be at home again, with peace declared.

Captain Godfrey, absolute though his power over us was – he could have ordered us all home at a moment's notice – turned out to be a delightful young officer, who did everything in his power to make our way smooth and pleasant, and who was certainly as good a manager as I ever had or ever expect to have. He entered into the spirit of our tour, and it was plain to see that it would be a success from start to finish if it were within his power to make it so. He liked to call himself my manager, and took a great delight, indeed, in the whole experience. Well, it was a change for him, no doubt!

I had brought a piano with me, but no accompanist. That was not an oversight; it was a matter of deliberate choice. I had been told, before I left home, that I would have no difficulty in finding some one among the soldiers to accompany me. And that was true, as I soon found.

In fact, as I was to learn later, I could have recruited a full orchestra among the Tommies, and I would have had in my band, too, musicians of fame and great ability, far above the average theater orchestra. Oh, you must go to France to learn how every art and craft in Britain has done its part!

Aye, every sort of artist and artisan, men of every profession and trade, can be found in the British army. It has taken them all, like some great melting pot, and made them soldiers. I think, indeed, there is no calling that you could name that would not yield you a master hand from the ranks of the British army. And I am not talking of the officers alone, but of the great mass of Tommies. And so when I told Captain Godfrey I would be needing a good pianist to play my accompaniments, he just smiled.

"Right you are!" he said. "We'll turn one up for you in no time!"

He had no doubts at all, and he was right. They found a lad called Johnson, a Yorkshireman, in a convalescent ward of one of the big hospitals. He was recovering from an illness he had incurred in the trenches, and was not quite ready to go back to active duty. But he was well enough to play for me, and delighted when he heard he might get the assignment. He was nervous lest he should not please me, and feared I might ask for another man. But when I ran over with him the songs I meant to sing I found he played the piano very well indeed, and had a knack for accompanying, too. There are good pianists, soloists, who are not good accompanists; it takes more than just the ability to play the piano to work with a singer, and especially with a singer like me. It is no straight ahead singing I do always, as you ken, perhaps.

But I saw at once that Johnson and I would get along fine together, so everyone was pleased, and I went on and made my preparations with him for my first concert. That was to be in the Boulogne Casino – center of the gayety of the resort in the old days, but now, for a long time, turned into a base hospital.

They had played for high stakes there in the old days before the war. Thousands of dollars had changed hands in an hour there. But they were playing for higher stakes now! They were playing for the lives and the health of men, and the hearts of the women at home in Britain who were bound up with them. In the old days men had staked their money against the turn of a card or the roll of the wheel. But now it was with Death they staked – and it was a mightier game than those old walls had ever seen before.

The largest ward of the hospital was in what had been the Baccarat room, and it was there I held my first concert of the trench engagement. When I appeared it was packed full. There were men on cots, lying still and helpless, bandaged to their very eyes. Some came limping in on their crutches; some were rolled in in chairs. It was a sad scene and an impressive one, and it went to my heart when I thought that my own poor laddie must have lain in just such a room – in this very one, perhaps. He had suffered as these men were suffering, and he had died – as some of these men for whom I was to sing would die. For there were men here who would be patched up, presently, and would go back. And for them there might be a next time – a next time when they would need no hospital.

There was one thing about the place I liked. It was so clean and white and spotless. All the garish display, the paint and tawdry finery, of the old gambling days, had gone. It was restful, now, and though there was the hospital smell, it was a clean smell. And the men looked as though they had wonderful care. Indeed, I knew they had that; I knew that everything that could be done to ease their state was being done. And every face I saw was brave and cheerful, though the skin of many and many a lad was stretched tight over his bones with the pain he had known, and there was a look in their eyes, a look with no repining in it, or complaint, but with the evidences of a terrible pain, bravely suffered, that sent the tears starting to my eyes more than once.

It was much as it had been in the many hospitals I had visited in Britain, and yet it was different, too. I felt that I was really at the front. Later I came to realize how far from the real front I actually was at Boulogne, but then I knew no better.

I had chosen my programme carefully. It was made up of songs altogether. I had had enough experience in hospitals and camps by now to have learned what soldiers liked best, and I had no doubt at all that it was just songs. And best of all they liked the old love songs, and the old songs of Scotland – tender, crooning melodies, that would help to carry them back, in memory, to their hames and, if they had them, to the lassies of their dreams. It was no sad, lugubrious songs they wanted. But a note of wistful tenderness they liked. That was true of sick and wounded, and of the hale and hearty too – and it showed that, though they were soldiers, they were just humans like the rest of us, for all the great and superhuman things they ha' done out there in France.

Not every actor and artist who has tried to help in the hospitals has fully understood the men he or she wanted to please. They meant well, every one, but some were a wee bit unfortunate in the way they went to work. There is a story that is told of one of our really great serious actors. He is serious minded, always, on the stage and off, and very, very dignified. But some folk went to him and asked him would he no do his bit to cheer up the puir laddies in a hospital?

He never thought of refusing – and I would no have you think I am sneering at the man! His intentions were of the best.

"Of course, I do not sing or dance," he said, drawing down his lip. And the look in his eyes showed what he thought of such of us as had descended to such low ways of pleasing the public that paid to see us and to hear us: "But I shall very gladly do something to bring a little diversion into the sad lives of the poor boys in the hospitals."

It was a stretcher audience that he had. That means a lot of boys who had to lie in bed to hear him. They needed cheering. And that great actor, with all his good intentions could think of nothing more fitting than to stand up before them and begin to recite, in a sad, elocutionary tone, Longfellow's "The Wreck of the Hesperus!"

He went on, and his voice gained power. He had come to the third stanza, or the fourth, maybe, when a command rang out through the ward. It was one that had been heard many and many a time in France, along the trenches. It came from one of the beds.

"To cover, men!" came the order.

It rang out through the ward, in a hoarse voice. And on the word every man's head popped under the bedclothes! And the great actor, astonished beyond measure, was left there, reciting away to shaking mounds of bedclothes that entrenched his hearers from the sound of his voice!

Well, I had heard yon tale. I do no think I should ever have risked a similar fate by making the same sort of mistake, but I profited by hearing it, and I always remembered it. And there was another thing. I never thought, when I was going to sing for soldiers, that I was doing something for them that should make them glad to listen to me, no matter what I chose to sing for them.

I always thought, instead, that here was an audience that had paid to hear me in the dearest coin in all the world – their legs and arms, their health and happiness. Oh, they had paid! They had not come in on free passes! Their tickets had cost them dear – dearer than tickets for the theater had ever cost before. I owed them more than I could ever pay – my own future, and my freedom, and the right and the chance to go on living in my own country free from the threat and the menace of the Hun. It was for me to please those boys when I sang for them, and to make such an effort as no ordinary audience had ever heard from me.

They had made a little platform to serve as a stage for me. There was room for me and for Johnson, and for the wee piano. And so I sang for them, and they showed me from the start that they were pleased. Those who could, clapped, and all cheered, and after each song there was a great pounding of crutches on the floor. It was an inspiring sound and a great sight, sad though it was to see and to hear.

When I had done I went aboot amang the men, shaking hands with such as could gie me their hands, and saying a word or two to all of them. Directly in front of the platform there lay a wounded Scots soldier, and all through my concert he watched me most intently; he never took his eyes off me. When I had sung my last song he beckoned to me feebly, and I went to him, and bent over to listen to him.

"Eh, Harry, man," he said, "will ye be doin' me a favor?"

"Aye, that I will, if I can," I told him.

"It's to ask the doctor will I no be gettin' better soon. Because, Harry, mon, I've but the one desire left – and that's to be in at the finish of yon fight!"

I was to give one more concert in Boulogne, that night. That was more cheerful, and it was different, again, from anything I had done or known before. There was a convalescent camp, about two miles from town, high up on the chalk cliffs. And this time my theater was a Y.M.C.A. hut. But do not let the name hut deceive ye! I had an audience of two thousand men that nicht! It was all the "hut" would hold, with tight squeezing. And what a roaring, wild crowd that was, to be sure! They sang with me, and they cheered and clapped until I thought that hut would be needing a new roof!

I had to give over at last, for I was tired, and needed sleep. We had our orders. The Reverend Harry Lauder, M.P., Tour was to start for Vimy Ridge at six o'clock next morning!

CHAPTER XIV

We were up next morning before daybreak. But I did not feel as if I were getting up early. Indeed, it was quite the reverse. All about us was a scene of such activity that I felt as if I had been lying in bed unconsciously long – as if I were the laziest man in all that busy town. Troops were setting out, boarding military trains. Cheery, jovial fellows they were – the same lads, some of them, who had crossed the Channel with me, and many others who had come in later. Oh, it is a steady stream of men and supplies, indeed, that goes across the narrow sea to France!

Motor trucks – they were calling them camions, after the French fashion, because it was a shorter and a simpler word – fairly swarmed in the streets. Guns rolled ponderously along. It was not military pomp we saw. Indeed, I saw little enough of that in France. It was only the uniforms and the guns that made me realize that this was war. The activity was more that of a busy, bustling factory town. It was not English, and it was not French. I think it made me think more of an American city. War, I cannot tell you often enough, is a great business, a vast industry, in these days. Someone said, and he was right, that they did not win victories any more – that they manufactured them, as all sorts of goods are manufactured. Digging, and building – that is the great work of modern war.

Our preparations, being in the hands of Captain Godfrey and the British army, were few and easily made. Two great, fast army motor cars had been put at the disposal of the Reverend Harry Lauder, M.P., Tour, and when we went out to get into them and make our start it was just a problem of stowing away all we had to carry with us.

The first car was a passenger car. Each motor had a soldier as chauffeur. I and the Reverend George Adam rode in the tonneau of the leading car, and Captain Godfrey, our manager and guide, sat with the driver, in front. That was where he belonged, and where, being a British officer, he naturally wanted to be. They have called our officers reckless, and said that they risked their lives too freely. Weel – I dinna ken! I am no soldier. But I know what a glorious tradition the British officer has – and I know, too, how his men follow him. They know, do the laddies in the ranks, that their officers will never ask them to go anywhere or do anything they would shirk themselves – and that makes for a spirit that you could not esteem too highly.

It was the second car that was our problem. We put Johnson, my accompanist, in the tonneau first, and then we covered him with cigarettes. It was a problem to get them stowed away, and when we had accomplished the task, finally, there was not much of Johnson to be seen! He was covered and surrounded with cigarettes, but he was snug, and he looked happy and comfortable, as he grinned at us – his face was about all of him that we could see. Hogge rode in front with the driver of that car, and had more room, so, than he would have had in the tonneau, where, as a passenger and a guest, he really belonged. The wee bit piano was lashed to the grid of the second car. And I give you my word it looked like a gypsy's wagon more than like one of the neat cars of the British army!

Weel, all was ready in due time, and it was just six o'clock when we set off. There was a thing I noted again and again. The army did things on time in France. If we were to start at a certain time we always did. Nothing ever happened to make us unpunctual.

It was a glorious morning! We went roaring out of Boulogne on a road that was as hard and smooth as a paved street in London despite all the terrific traffic it had borne since the war made Boulogne a British base. And there were no speed limits here. So soon as the cars were tuned up we went along at the highest speed of which the cars were capable. Our soldier drivers knew their business; only the picked men were assigned to the driving of these cars, and speed was one of the things that was wanted of them. Much may hang on the speed of a motor car in France.

But, fast as we traveled, we did not go too fast for me to enjoy the drive and the sights and sounds that were all about us. They were oddly mixed. Some were homely and familiar, and some were so strange that I could not give over wondering at them. The motors made a great noise, but it was not too loud for me to hear larks singing in the early morning. All the world was green with the early sun upon it, lighting up every detail of a strange countryside. There was a soft wind, a gentle, caressing wind, that stirred the leaves of the trees along the road.

But not for long could we escape the touch of war. That grim etcher was at work upon the road and the whole countryside. As we went on we were bound to move more slowly, because of the congestion of the traffic. Never was Piccadilly or Fifth Avenue more crowded with motors at the busiest hour of the day than was that road. As we passed through villages or came to cross roads we saw military police, directing traffic, precisely as they do at busy intersections of crowded streets in London or New York.

But the traffic along that road was not the traffic of the cities. Here were no ladies, gorgeously clad, reclining in their luxurious, deeply upholstered cars. Here were no footmen and chauffeurs in livery. Ah, they wore a livery – aye! But it was the livery of glory – the khaki of the King! Generals and high officers passed us, bowling along, lolling in their cars, taking their few brief minutes or half hours of ease, smoking and talking. They corresponded to the limousines and landaulets of the cities. And there were wagons from the shops – great trucks, carrying supplies, going along at a pace that racked their engines and their bodies, and that boded disaster to whoever got in their way. But no one did – there was no real confusion here, despite the seeming madness of the welter of traffic that we saw.

What a traffic that was! And it was all the traffic of the carnage we were nearing. It was a marvelous and an impressive panorama of force and of destruction that we saw it was being constantly unrolled before my wondering eyes as we traveled along the road out of old Boulogne.

At first all the traffic was going our way. Sometimes there came a warning shriek from behind, and everything drew to one side to make room for a dispatch rider on a motor cycle. These had the right of way. Sir Douglas Haig himself, were he driving along, would see his driver turn out to make way for one of those shrieking motor bikes! The rule is absolute – everything makes way for them.

But it was not long before a tide of traffic began to meet us, flowing back toward Boulogne. There was a double stream then, and I wondered how collisions and traffic jams of all sorts could be avoided. I do not know yet; I only know that there is no trouble. Here were empty trucks, speeding back for new loads. And some there were that carried all sorts of wreckage – the flotsam and jetsam cast up on the safe shores behind the front by the red tide of war. Nothing is thrown away out there; nothing is wasted. Great piles of discarded shoes are brought back to be made over. They are as good as new when they come back from the factories where they are worked over. Indeed, the men told me they were better than new, because they were less trying to their feet, and did not need so much breaking in.

Men go about, behind the front, and after a battle, picking up everything that has been thrown away. Everything is sorted and gone over with the utmost care. Rifles that have been thrown away or dropped when men were wounded or killed, bits of uniforms, bayonets – everything is saved. Reclamation is the order of the day. There is waste enough in war that cannot be avoided; the British army sees to it that there is none that is avoidable.

But it was not only that sort of wreckage, that sort of driftwood that was being carried back to be made over. Presently we began to see great motor ambulances coming along, each with a Red Cross painted glaringly on its side – though that paint was wasted or worse, for there is no target the Hun loves better, it would seem, than the great red cross of mercy. And in them, as we knew, there was the most pitiful wreckage of all – the human wreckage of the war.

In the wee sma' hours of the morn they bear the men back who have been hit the day before and during the night. They go back to the field dressing stations and the hospitals just behind the front, to be sorted like the other wreckage. Some there are who cannot be moved further, at first, but must he cared for under fire, lest they die on the way. But all whose wounds are such that they can safely be moved go back in the ambulances, first to the great base hospitals, and then, when possible, on the hospital ships to England.

Sometimes, but not often, we passed troops marching along the road. They swung along. They marched easily, with the stride that could carry them furthest with the least effort. They did not look much like the troops I used to see in London. They did not have the snap of the Coldstream Guards, marching through Green Park in the old days. But they looked like business and like war.

They looked like men who had a job of work to do and meant to see it through.

They had discipline, those laddies, but it was not the old, stiff discipline of the old army. That is a thing of a day that is dead and gone. Now, as we passed along the side of the road that marching troops always leave clear, there was always a series of hails for me.

"Hello, Harry!" I would hear.

And I would look back, and see grinning Tommies waving their hands to me. It was a flattering experience, I can tell you, to be recognized like that along that road. It was like running into old friends in a strange town where you have come thinking you know no one at all.

We were about thirty miles out of Boulogne when there was a sudden explosion underneath the car, followed by a sibilant sound that I knew only too well.

"Hello – a puncture!" said Godfrey, and smiled as he turned around. We drew up to the side of the road, and both chauffeurs jumped out and went to work on the recalcitrant tire. The rest of us sat still, and gazed around us at the fields. I was glad to have a chance to look quietly about. The fields stretched out, all emerald green, in all directions to the distant horizon, sapphire blue that glorious morning. And in the fields, here and there, were the bent, stooped figures of old men and women. They were carrying on, quietly. Husbands and sons and brothers had gone to war; all the young men of France had gone. These were left, and they were seeing to the performance of the endless cycle of duty. France would survive; the Hun could not crush her. Here was a spirit made manifest – a spirit different in degree but not in kind from the spirit of my ain Britain. It brought a lump into my throat to see them, the old men and the women, going so patiently and quietly about their tasks.

It was very quiet. Faint sounds came to us; there was a distant rumbling, like the muttering of thunder on a summer's night, when the day has been hot and there are low, black clouds lying against the horizon, with the flashes of the lightning playing through them. But that I had come already not to heed, though I knew full well, by now, what it was and what it meant. For a little space the busy road had become clear; there was a long break in the traffic.

I turned to Adam and to Captain Godfrey.

"I'm thinking here's a fine chance for a bit of a rehearsal in the open air," I said. "I'm not used to singing so – mayhap it would be well to try my voice and see will it carry as it should."

"Right oh!" said Godfrey.

And so we dug Johnson out from his snug barricade of cigarettes, that hid him as an emplacement hides a gun, and we unstrapped my wee piano, and set it up in the road. Johnson tried the piano, and then we began.

I think I never sang with less restraint in all my life than I did that quiet morning on the Boulogne road. I raised my voice and let it have its will. And I felt my spirits rising with the lilt of the melody. My voice rang out, full and free, and it must have carried far and wide across the fields.

My audience was small at first – Captain Godfrey, Hogge, Adam, and the two chauffeurs, working away, and having more trouble with the tire than they had thought at first they would – which is the way of tires, as every man knows who owns a car. But as they heard my songs the old men and women in the fields straightened up to listen. They stood wondering, at first, and then, slowly, they gave over their work for a space, and came to gather round me and to listen.

It must have seemed strange to them! Indeed, it must have seemed strange to anyone had they seen and heard me! There I was, with Johnson at my piano, like some wayside tinker setting up his cart and working at his trade! But I did not care for appearances – not a whit. For the moment I was care free, a wandering minstrel, like some troubadour of old, care free and happy in my song. I forgot the black shadow under which we all lay in that smiling land, the black shadow of war in which I sang.

It delighted me to see those old peasants and to study their faces, and to try to win them with my song. They could not understand a word I sang, and yet I saw the smiles breaking out over their wrinkled faces, and it made me proud and happy. For it was plain that I was reaching them – that I was able to throw a bridge over the gap of a strange tongue and an alien race. When I had done and it was plain I meant to sing no more they clapped me.

"There's a hand for you, Harry," said Adam. "Aye – and I'm proud of it!" I told him for reply.

I was almost sorry when I saw that the two chauffeurs had finished their repairs and were ready to go on. But I told them to lash the piano back in its place, and Johnson prepared to climb gingerly back among his cigarettes. But just then something happened that I had not expected.

There was a turn in the road just beyond us that hid its continuation from us. And around the bend now there came a company of soldiers. Not neat and well-appointed soldiers these. Ah, no! They were fresh from the trenches, on their way back to rest. The mud and grime of the trenches were upon them. They were tired and weary, and they carried all their accoutrements and packs with them. Their boots were heavy with mud. And they looked bad, and many of them shaky. Most of these men, Godfrey told me after a glance at them, had been ordered back to hospital for minor ailments. They were able to march, but not much more.

They were the first men I had seen in such a case, They looked bad enough, but Godfrey said they were happy enough. Some of them would get leave for Blighty, and be home, in a few days, to see their families and their girls. And they came swinging along in fine style, sick and tired as they were, for the thought of where they were going cheered them and helped to keep them going.

A British soldier, equipped for the trenches, on his way in or out, has quite a load to carry. He has his pack, and his emergency ration, and his entrenching tools, and extra clothing that he needs in bad weather in the trenches, to say nothing of his ever-present rifle. And the sight of them made me realize for the first time the truth that lay behind the jest in a story that is one of Tommy's favorites.

A child saw a soldier in heavy marching order. She gazed at him in wide-eyed wonder. He was not her idea of what a soldier should look like.

"Mother," she asked, "what is a soldier for?"

The mother gazed at the man. And then she smiled.

"A soldier," she answered, "is to hang things on."

They eyed me very curiously as they came along, those sick laddies. They couldn't seem to understand what I was doing there, but their discipline held them. They were in charge of a young lieutenant with one star – a second lieutenant. I learned later that he was a long way from being a well man himself. So I stopped him.

"Would your men like to hear a few songs, lieutenant?" I asked him.

He hesitated. He didn't quite understand, and he wasn't a bit sure what his duty was in the circumstances. He glanced at Godfrey, and Godfrey smiled at him as if in encouragement.

"It's very good of you, I'm sure," he said, slowly. "Fall out!"

So the men fell out, and squatted there, along the wayside. At once discipline was relaxed. Their faces were a study as the wee piano was set up again, and Johnson, in uniform, of course sat down and tried a chord or two. And then suddenly something happened that broke the ice. Just as I stood up to sing a loud voice broke the silence.

"Lor' love us!" one of the men cried, "if it ain't old 'Arry Lauder!"

There was a stir of interest at once. I spotted the owner of the voice. It was a shriveled up little chap, with a weazened face that looked like a sun-dried apple. He was showing all his teeth in a grin at me, and he was a typical little cockney of the sort all Londoners know well.

"Go it, 'Arry!" he shouted, shrilly. "Many's the time h' I've 'eard you at the old Shoreditch!"

So I went it as well as I could, and I never did have a more appreciative audience. My little cockney friend seemed to take a particular personal pride in me. I think he thought he had found me, and that he was, in an odd way, responsible for my success with his mates. And so he was especially glad when they cheered me and thanked me as they did.

My concert didn't last long, for we had to be getting on, and the company of sick men had just so much time, too, to reach their destination – Boulogne, whence we had set out. When it was over I said good-by to the men, and shook hands with particular warmth with the little cockney. It wasn't every day I was likely to meet a man who had often heard me at the old Shoreditch! After we had stowed Johnson and the piano away again, with a few less cigarettes, now, to get in Johnson's way, we started, and as long as we were in sight the little cockney and I were waving to one another.

I took some of the cigarettes into the car I was in now. And as we sped along we were again in the thick of the great British war machine. Motor trucks and ambulances were more frequent than ever, and it was a common occurrence now to pass soldiers, marching in both directions – to the front and away from it. There was always someone to recognize me and start a volley of "Hello, Harrys" coming my way, and I answered every greeting, you may be sure, and threw cigarettes to go with my "Hellos."

Aye, I was glad I had brought the cigarettes! They seemed to be even more welcome than I had hoped they would be, and I only wondered how long the supply would hold out, and if I would be able to get more if it did not. So Johnson, little by little, was getting more room, as I called for more and more of the cigarettes that walled him in in his tonneau.

About noon, as we drove through a little town, I saw, for the first time, a whole flock of airplanes riding the sky. They were swooping about like lazy hawks, and a bonnie sight they were. I drew a long breath when I saw them, and turned to my friend Adam.

"Well," I said, "I think we're coming to it, now!"

I meant the front – the real, British front.

Suddenly, at a sharp order from Captain Godfrey, our cars stopped. He turned around to us, and grinned, very cheerfully.

"Gentlemen," he said, very calmly, "we'll stop here long enough to put on our steel helmets."

He said it just as he might have said: "Well, here's where we will stop for tea."

It meant no more than that to him. But for me it meant many things. It meant that at last I was really to be under fire; that I was going into danger. I was not really frightened yet; you have to see danger, and know just what it is, and appreciate exactly its character, before you can be frightened. But I had imagination enough to know what that order meant, and to have a queer feeling as I donned the steel helmet. It was less uncomfortable than I had expected it to be – lighter, and easier to wear. The British trench helmets are beautifully made, now; as in every other phase of the war and its work they represent a constant study for improvement, lightening.

But, even had it not been for the warning that was implied in Captain Godfrey's order, I should soon have understood that we had come into a new region. For a long time now the noise of the guns had been different. Instead of being like distant thunder it was a much nearer and louder sound. It was a steady, throbbing roar now.

And, at intervals, there came a different sound; a sound more individual, that stood out from the steady roar. It was as if the air were being cracked apart by the blow of some giant hammer. I knew what it was. Aye, I knew. You need no man to tell you what it is – the explosion of a great shell not so far from you!

Nor was it our ears alone that told us what was going on. Ever and anon, now, ahead of us, as we looked at the fields, we saw a cloud of dirt rise up. That was where a shell struck. And in the fields about us, now, we could see holes, full of water, as a rule, and mounds of dirt that did not look as if shovels and picks had raised them.

It surprised me to see that the peasants were still at work. I spoke to Godfrey about that.

"The French peasants don't seem to know what it is to be afraid of shell-fire," he said. "They go only when we make them. It is the same on the French front. They will cling to a farmhouse in the zone of fire until they are ordered out, no matter how heavily it may be shelled. They are splendid folk! The Germans can never beat a race that has such folk as that behind its battle line."

I could well believe him. I have seen no sight along the whole front more quietly impressive than the calm, impassive courage of those French peasants. They know they are right! It is no Kaiser, no war lord, who gives them courage. It is the knowledge and the consciousness that they are suffering in a holy cause, and that, in the end, the right and the truth must prevail. Their own fate, whatever may befall them, does not matter. France must go on and shall, and they do their humble part to see that she does and shall.

Solemn thoughts moved me as we drove on. Here there had been real war and fighting. Now I saw a country blasted by shell-fire and wrecked by the contention of great armies. And I knew that I was coming to soil watered by British blood; to rows of British graves; to soil that shall be forever sacred to the memory of the Britons, from Britain and from over the seas, who died and fought upon it to redeem it from the Hun.

I had no mind to talk, to ask questions. For the time I was content to be with my own thoughts, that were evoked by the historic ground through which we passed. My heart was heavy with grief and with the memories of my boy that came flooding it, but it was lightened, too, by other thoughts.

And always, as we sped on, there was the thunder of the guns. Always there were the bursting shells, and the old bent peasants paying no heed to them. Always there were the circling airplanes, far above us, like hawks against the deep blue of the sky. And always we came nearer and nearer to Vimy Ridge – that deathless name in the history of Britain.

CHAPTER XV

Now Captain Godfrey leaned back and smiled at us.

"There's Vimy Ridge," he said. And he pointed.

"Yon?" I asked, in astonishment.

I was almost disappointed. We had heard so much, in Britain and in Scotland, of Vimy Ridge. The name of that famous hill had been written imperishably in history. But to look at it first, to see it as I saw it, it was no hill at all! My eyes were used to the mountains of my ain Scotland, and this great ridge was but a tiny thing beside them. But then I began to picture the scene as it had been the day the Canadians stormed it and won for themselves the glory of all the ages. I pictured it blotted from sight by the hell of shells bursting over it, and raking its slopes as the Canadians charged upward. I pictured it crowned by defenses and lined by such of the Huns as had survived the artillery battering, spitting death and destruction from their machine guns. And then I saw it as I should, and I breathed deep at the thought of the men who had faced death and hell to win that height and plant the flag of Britain upon it. Aye, and the Stars and Stripes of America, too!

Ye ken that tale? There was an American who had enlisted, like so many of his fellow countrymen before America was in the war, in the Canadian forces. The British army was full of men who had told a white lie to don the King's uniform. Men there are in the British army who winked as they enlisted and were told: "You'll be a Canadian?"

"Aye, aye, I'm a Canadian," they'd say.

"From what province?"

"The province of Kentucky – or New York – or California!"

Well, there was a lad, one of them, was in the first wave at Vimy Ridge that April day in 1917. 'Twas but a few days before that a wave of the wildest cheering ever heard had run along the whole Western front, so that Fritz in his trenches wondered what was up the noo. Well, he has learned, since then! He has learned, despite his Kaiser and his officers, and his lying newspapers, that that cheer went up when the news came that America had declared war upon Germany. And so, it was a few days after that cheer was heard that the Canadians leaped over the top and went for Vimy Ridge, and this young fellow from America had a wee silken flag. He spoke to his officer.

"Now that my own country's in the war, sir," he said, "I'd like to carry her flag with me when we go over the top. Wrapped around me, sir – "

"Go it!" said the officer.

And so he did. And he was one of those who won through and reached the top. There he was wounded, but he had carried the Stars and Stripes with him to the crest.

Vimy Ridge! I could see it. And above it, and beyond it, now, for the front had been carried on, far beyond, within what used to be the lines of the Hun, the airplanes circled. Very quiet and lazy they seemed, for all I knew of their endless activity and the precious work that they were doing. I could see how the Huns were shelling them. You would see an airplane hovering, and then, close by, suddenly, a ball of cottony white smoke. Shrapnel that was, bursting, as Fritz tried to get the range with an anti-aircraft gun – an Archie, as the Tommies call them. But the plane would pay no heed, except, maybe, to dip a bit or climb a little higher to make it harder for the Hun. It made me think of a man shrugging his shoulders, calmly and imperturbably, in the face of some great peril, and I wanted to cheer. I had some wild idea that maybe he would hear me, and know that someone saw him, and appreciated what he was doing – someone to whom it was not an old story! But then I smiled at my own thought.

Now it was time for us to leave the cars and get some exercise. Our steel helmets were on, and glad we were of them, for shrapnel was bursting nearby sometimes, although most of the shells were big fellows, that buried themselves in the ground and then exploded. Fritz wasn't doing much casual shelling the noo, though. He was saving his fire until his observers gave him a real target to aim at. But that was no so often, for our airplanes were in command of the air then, and his flyers got precious little chance to guide his shooting. Most of his hits were due to luck.

"Spread out a bit as you go along here," said Captain Godfrey. "If a crump lands close by there's no need of all of us going! If we're spread out a bit, you see, a shell might get one and leave the rest of us."

It sounded cold blooded, but it was not. To men who have lived at the front everything comes to be taken as a matter of course. Men can get used to anything – this war has proved that again, if there was need of proving it. And I came to understand that, and to listen to things I heard with different ears. But those are things no one can tell you of; you must have been at the front yourself to understand all that goes on there, both in action and in the minds of men.

We obeyed Captain Godfrey readily enough, as you can guess. And so I was alone as I walked toward Vimy Ridge. It looked just like a lumpy excrescence on the landscape; at hame we would not even think of it as a foothill. But as I neared it, and as I remembered all it stood for, I thought that in the atlas of history it would loom higher than the highest peak of the great Himalaya range.

Beyond the ridge, beyond the actual line of the trenches, miles away, indeed, were the German batteries from which the shells we heard and saw as they burst were coming. I was glad of my helmet, and of the cool assurance of Captain Godfrey. I felt that we were as safe, in his hands, as men could be in such a spot.

It was not more than a mile we had to cover, but it was rough going, bad going. Here war had had its grim way without interruption. The face of the earth had been cut to pieces. Its surface had been smashed to a pulpy mass. The ground had been plowed, over and over, by a rain of shells – German and British. What a planting there had been that spring, and what a plowing! A harvest of death it had been that had been sown – and the reaper had not waited for summer to come, and the Harvest moon. He had passed that way with his scythe, and where we passed now he had taken his terrible, his horrid, toll.

At the foot of the ridge I saw men fighting for the first time – actually fighting, seeking to hurt an enemy. It was a Canadian battery we saw, and it was firing, steadily and methodically, at the Huns. Up to now I had seen only the vast industrial side of war, its business and its labor. Now I was, for the first time, in touch with actual fighting. I saw the guns belching death and destruction, destined for men miles away. It was high angle fire, of course, directed by observers in the air.

But even that seemed part of the sheer, factory-like industry of war. There was no passion, no coming to grips in hot blood, here. Orders were given by the battery commander and the other officers as the foreman in a machine shop might give them. And the busy artillerymen worked like laborers, too, clearing their guns after a salvo, loading them, bringing up fresh supplies of ammunition. It was all methodical, all a matter of routine.

"Good artillery work is like that," said Captain Godfrey, when I spoke to him about it. "It's a science. It's all a matter of the higher mathematics. Everything is worked out to half a dozen places of decimals. We've eliminated chance and guesswork just as far as possible from modern artillery actions."

But there was something about it all that was disappointing, at first sight. It let you down a bit. Only the guns themselves kept up the tradition. Only they were acting as they should, and showing a proper passion and excitement. I could hear them growling ominously, like dogs locked in their kennel when they would be loose and about, and hunting. And then they would spit, angrily. They inflamed my imagination, did those guns; they satisfied me and my old-fashioned conception of war and fighting, more than anything else that I had seen had done. And it seemed to me that after they had spit out their deadly charge they wiped their muzzles with red tongues of flame, satisfied beyond all words or measure with what they had done.

We were rising now, as we walked, and getting a better view of the country that lay beyond. And so I came to understand a little better the value of a height even so low and insignificant as Vimy Ridge in that flat country. While the Germans held it they could overlook all our positions, and all the advantage of natural placing had been to them. Now, thanks to the Canadians, it was our turn, and we were looking down.

Weel, I was under fire. There was no doubt about it. There was a droning over us now, like the noise bees make, or many flies in a small room on a hot summer's day. That was the drone of the German shells. There was a little freshening of the artillery activity on both sides, Captain Godfrey said, as if in my honor. When one side increased its fire the other always answered – played copy cat. There was no telling, ye ken, when such an increase of fire might not be the first sign of an attack. And neither side took more chances than it must.

I had known, before I left Britain, that I would come under fire. And I had wondered what it would be like: I had expected to be afraid, nervous. Brave men had told me, one after another, that every man is afraid when he first comes under fire. And so I had wondered how I would be, and I had expected to be badly scared and extremely nervous. Now I could hear that constant droning of shells, and, in the distance, I could see, very often, powdery squirts of smoke and dirt along the ground, where our shells were striking, so that I knew I had the Hun lines in sight.

And I can truthfully say that, that day, at least, I felt no great fear or nervousness. Later I did, as I shall tell you, but that day one overpowering emotion mastered every other. It was a desire for vengeance! You were the Huns – the men who had killed my boy. They were almost within my reach. And as I looked at them there in their lines a savage desire possessed me, almost overwhelmed me, indeed, that made me want to rush to those guns and turn them to my own mad purpose of vengeance.

It was all I could do, I tell you, to restrain myself – to check that wild, almost ungovernable impulse to rush to the guns and grapple with them myself – myself fire them at the men who had killed my boy. I wanted to fight! I wanted to fight with my two hands – to tear and rend, and have the consciousness that I flash back, like a telegraph message from my satiated hands to my eager brain that was spurring me on.

But that was not to be. I knew it, and I grew calmer, presently. The roughness of the going helped me to do that, for it took all a man's wits and faculties to grope his way along the path we were following now. Indeed, it was no path at all that led us to the Pimple – the topmost point of Vimy Ridge, which changed hands half a dozen times in the few minutes of bloody fighting that had gone on here during the great attack.

The ground was absolutely riddled with shell holes here. There must have been a mine of metal underneath us. What path there was zigzagged around. It had been worn to such smoothness as it possessed since the battle, and it evaded the worst craters by going around them. My madness was passed now, and a great sadness had taken its place. For here, where I was walking, men had stumbled up with bullets and shells raining about them. At every step I trod ground that must have been the last resting-place of some Canadian soldier, who had died that I might climb this ridge in a safety so immeasurably greater than his had been.

If it was hard for us to make this climb, if we stumbled as we walked, what had it been for them? Our breath came hard and fast – how had it been with them? Yet they had done it! They had stormed the ridge the Huns had proudly called impregnable. They had taken, in a swift rush, that nothing could stay, a position the Kaiser's generals had assured him would never be lost – could never be reached by mortal troops.

The Pimple, for which we were heading now, was an observation post at that time. There there was a detachment of soldiers, for it was an important post, covering much of the Hun territory beyond. A major of infantry was in command; his headquarters were a large hole in the ground, dug for him by a German shell – fired by German gunners who had no thought further from their minds than to do a favor for a British officer. And he was sitting calmly in front of his headquarters, smoking a pipe, when we reached the crest and came to the Pimple.

He was a very calm man, that major, given, I should say, to the greatest repression. I think nothing would have moved him from that phlegmatic calm of his! He watched us coming, climbing and making hard going of it. If he was amused he gave no sign, as he puffed at his pipe. I, for one, was puffing, too – I was panting like a grampus. I had thought myself in good condition, but I found out at Vimy Ridge that I was soft and flabby.

Not a sign did that major give until we reached him. And then, as we stood looking at him, and beyond him at the panorama of the trenches, he took his pipe from his mouth.

"Welcome to Vimy Ridge!" he said, in the manner of a host greeting a party bidden for the weekend.

I was determined that that major should not outdo me. I had precious little wind left to breathe with, much less to talk, but I called for the last of it.

"Thank you, major," I said. "May I join you in a smoke?"

"Of course you can!" he said, unsmiling.

"That is, if you've brought your pipe with you."

"Aye, I've my pipe," I told him. "I may forget to pay my debt, but I'll never forget my pipe." And no more I will.

So I sat down beside him, and drew out my pipe, and made a long business of filling it, and pushing the tobacco down just so, since that gave me a chance to get my wind. And when I was ready to light up I felt better, and I was breathing right, so that I could talk as I pleased without fighting for breath.

My friend the major proved an entertaining chap, and a talkative one, too, for all his seeming brusqueness. He pointed out the spots that had been made famous in the battle, and explained to me what it was the Canadians had done. And I saw and understood better than ever before what a great feat that had been, and how heavily it had counted. He lent me his binoculars, too, and with them I swept the whole valley toward Lens, where the great French coal mines are, and where the Germans have been under steady fire so long, and have been hanging on by their eyelashes.

It was not the place I should choose, ordinarily, to do a bit of sight-seeing. The German shells were still humming through the air above us, though not quite so often as they had. But there were enough of them, and they seemed to me close enough for me to feel the wind they raised as they passed. I thought for sure one of them would come along, presently, and clip my ears right off. And sometimes I felt myself ducking my head – as if that would do me any good! But I did not think about it; I would feel myself doing it, without having intended to do anything of the sort. I was a bit nervous, I suppose, but no one could be really scared or alarmed in the unplumbable depths of calm in which that British major was plunged!

It was a grand view I had of the valley, but it was not the sort of thing I had expected to see. I knew there were thousands of men there, and I think I had expected to see men really fighting. But there was nothing of the sort. Not a man could I see in all the valley. They were under cover, of course. When I stopped to think about it, that was what I should have expected, of course. If I could have seen our laddies there below, why, the Huns could have seen them too. And that would never have done.

I could hear our guns, too, now, very well. They were giving voice all around me, but never a gun could I see, for all my peering and searching around. Even the battery we had passed below was out of sight now. And it was a weird thing, and an uncanny thing to think of all that riot of sound around, and not a sight to be had of the batteries that were making it!

Hogge came up while I was talking to the major. "Hello!" he said. "What have you done to your knee, Lauder?"

I looked down and saw a trickle of blood running down, below my knee. It was bare, of course, because I wore my kilt.

"Oh, that's nothing," I said.

I knew at once what it was. I remembered that, as I stumbled up the hill, I had tripped over a bit of barbed wire and scratched my leg. And so I explained.

"And I fell into a shell-hole, too," I said. "A wee one, as they go around here." But I laughed. "Still, I'll be able to say I was wounded on Vimy Ridge."

I glanced at the major as I said that, and was half sorry I had made the poor jest. And I saw him smile, in one corner of his mouth, as I said I had been "wounded." It was the corner furthest from me, but I saw it. And it was a dry smile, a withered smile. I could guess his thought.

"Wounded!" he must have said to himself, scornfully. And he must have remembered the real wounds the Canadians had received on that hillside. Aye, I could guess his thought. And I shared it, although I did not tell him so. But I think he understood.

He was still sitting there, puffing away at his old pipe, as quiet and calm and imperturbable as ever, when Captain Godfrey gathered us together to go on. He gazed out over the valley.

He was a man to be remembered for a long time, that major. I can see him now, in my mind's eye, sitting there, brooding, staring out toward Lens and the German lines. And I think that if I were choosing a figure for some great sculptor to immortalize, to typify and represent the superb, the majestic imperturbability of the British Empire in time of stress and storm, his would be the one. I could think of no finer figure than his for such a statue. You would see him, if the sculptor followed my thought, sitting in front of his shell-hole on Vimy Ridge, calm, dispassionate, devoted to his duty and the day's work, quietly giving the directions that guided the British guns in their work of blasting the Hun out of the refuge he had chosen when the Canadians had driven him from the spot where the major sat.

It was easier going down Vimy Ridge than it had been coming up, but it was hard going still. We had to skirt great, gaping holes torn by monstrous shells – shells that had torn the very guts out of the little hill.

"We're going to visit another battery," said Captain Godfrey. "I'll tell you I think it's the best hidden battery on the whole British front! And that's saying a good deal, for we've learned a thing or two about hiding our whereabouts from Fritz. He's a curious one, Fritz is, but we try not to gratify his curiosity any more than we must."

"I'll be glad to see more of the guns," I said.

"Well, here you'll see more than guns. The major in command at this battery we're heading for has a decoration that was given to him just for the way he hid his guns. There's much more than fighting that a man has to do in this war if he's to make good."

As we went along I kept my eyes open, trying to get a peep at the guns before Godfrey should point them out to me. I could hear firing going on all around me, but there was so much noise that my ears were not a guide. I was not a trained observer, of course; I would not know a gun position at sight, as some soldier trained to the work would be sure to do. And yet I thought I could tell when I was coming to a great battery. I thought so, I say!

Again, though I had that feeling of something weird and uncanny. For now, as we walked along, I did hear the guns, and I was sure, from the nature of the sound, that we were coming close to them. But, as I looked straight toward the spot where my ears told me that they must be, I could see nothing at all. I thought that perhaps Godfrey had lost his way, and that we were wandering along the wrong path. It did not seem likely, but it was possible.

And then, suddenly, when I was least expecting it, we stopped.

"Well – here we are!" said the captain, and grinned at our amazement. And there we were indeed! We were right among the guns of a Canadian battery, and the artillerymen were shouting their welcome, for they had heard that I was coming, and recognized me as soon as they saw me. But – how had we got here? I looked around me, in utter amazement. Even now that I had come to the battery I could not understand how it was that I had been deceived – how that battery had been so marvelously concealed that, if one did not know of its existence and of its exact location, one might literally stumble over it in broad daylight!

CHAPTER XVI

It had turned very hot, now, at the full of the day. Indeed, it was grilling weather, and there in the battery, in a hollow, close down beside a little run or stream, it was even hotter than on the shell-swept bare top of the ridge. So the Canadian gunners had stripped down for comfort. Not a man had more than his under-shirt on above his trousers, and many of them were naked to the waist, with their hide tanned to the color of old saddles.

These laddies reminded me of those in the first battery I had seen. They were just as calm, and just as dispassionate as they worked in their mill – it might well have been a mill in which I saw them working. Only they were no grinding corn, but death – death for the Huns, who had brought death to so many of their mates. But there was no excitement, there were no cries of hatred and anger.

They were hard at work. Their work, it seemed, never came to an end or even to a pause. The orders rang out, in a sort of sing-song voice. After each shot a man who sat with a telephone strapped about his head called out corrections of the range, in figures that were just a meaningless jumble to me, although they made sense to the men who listened and changed the pointing of the guns at each order.

Their faces, that, like their bare backs and chests, looked like tanned leather, were all grimy from their work among the smoke and the gases. And through the grime the sweat had run down like little rivers making courses for themselves in the soft dirt of a hillside. They looked grotesque enough, but there was nothing about them to make me feel like laughing, I can tell you! And they all grinned amiably when the amazed and disconcerted Reverend Harry Lauder, M.P., Tour came tumbling in among them. We all felt right at hame at once – and I the more so when a chap I had met and come to know well in Toronto during one of my American tours came over and gripped my hand.

"Aye, but it's good to see your face, Harry!" he said, as he made me welcome.

This battery had done great work ever since it had come out. No battery in the whole army had a finer record, I was told. And no one needed to tell me the tale of its losses. Not far away there was a little cemetery, filled with doleful little crosses, set up over mounds that told their grim story all too plainly and too eloquently.

The battery had gone through the Battle of Vimy Ridge and made a great name for itself. And now it was set down upon a spot that had seen some of the very bloodiest of the fighting on that day. I saw here, for the first time, some of the most horrible things that the war holds. There was a little stream, as I said, that ran through the hollow in which the battery was placed, and that stream had been filled with blood, not water, on the day of the battle.

Everywhere, here, were whitened bones of men. In the wild swirling of the battle, and the confusion of digging in and meeting German counter attacks that had followed it, it had not been possible to bury all the dead. And so the whitened bones remained, though the elements had long since stripped them bare. The elements – and the hungry rats. These are not pretty things to tell, but they are true, and the world should know what war is to-day.

I almost trod upon one skeleton that remained complete. It was that of a huge German soldier – a veritable giant of a man, he must have been. The bones of his feet were still encased in his great boots, their soles heavily studded with nails. Even a few shreds of his uniform remained. But the flesh was all gone. The sun and the rats and the birds had accounted for the last morsel of it.

Hundreds of years from now, I suppose, the bones that were strewn along that ground will still be being turned up by plows. The generations to come who live there will never lack relics of the battle, and of the fighting that preceded and followed it. They will find bones, and shell cases, and bits of metal of all sorts. Rusty bayonets will be turned up by their plowshares; strange coins, as puzzling as some of those of Roman times that we in Britain have found, will puzzle them. Who can tell how long it will be before the soil about Vimy Ridge will cease to give up its relics?

That ground had been searched carefully for everything that might conceivably be put to use again, or be made fit for further service. The British army searches every battlefield so in these days. And yet, when I was there, many weeks after the storm of fighting had passed on, and when the scavengers had done their work, the ground was still rather thickly strewn with odds and ends that interested me vastly. I might have picked up much more than I did. But I could not carry so very much, and, too, so many of the things brought grisly thoughts to my mind! God knows I needed no reminders of the war! I had a reminder in my heart, that never left me. Still, I took some few things, more for the sake of the hame folks, who might not see, and would, surely, be interested. I gathered some bayonets for my collection – somehow they seemed the things I was most willing to take along. One was British, one German – two were French.

But the best souvenir of all I got at Vimy Ridge I did not pick up. It was given to me by my friend, the grave major – him of whom I would like some famous sculptor to make a statue as he sat at his work of observation. That was a club – a wicked looking instrument. This club had a great thick head, huge in proportion to its length and size, and this head was studded with great, sharp nails. A single blow from it would finish the strongest man that ever lived. It was a fit weapon for a murderer – and a murderer had wielded it. The major had taken it from a Hun, who had meant to use it – had, doubtless, used it! – to beat out the brains of wounded men, lying on the ground. Many of those clubs were taken from the Germans, all along the front, both by the British and the

French, and the Germans had never made any secret of the purpose for which they were intended. Well, they picked poor men to try such tactics on when they went against the Canadians!

The Canadians started no such work, but they were quick to adopt a policy of give and take. It was the Canadians who began the trench raids for which the Germans have such a fierce distaste, and after they had learned something of how Fritz fought the Canadians took to paying him back in some of his own coin. Not that they matched the deeds of the Huns – only a Hun could do that. But the Canadians were not eager to take prisoners. They would bomb a dugout rather than take its occupants back. And a dugout that has been bombed yields few living men!

Who shall blame them? Not I – nor any other man who knows what lessons in brutality and treachery the Canadians have had from the Hun. It was the Canadians, near Ypres, who went through the first gas attack – that fearful day when the Germans were closer to breaking through than they ever were before or since. I shall not set down here all the tales I heard of the atrocities of the Huns. Others have done that. Men have written of that who have firsthand knowledge, as mine cannot be. I know only what has been told to me, and there is little need of hearsay evidence. There is evidence enough that any court would accept as hanging proof. But this much it is right to say – that no troops along the Western front have more to revenge than have the Canadians.

It is not the loss of comrades, dearly loved though they be, that breeds hatred among the soldiers. That is a part of war, and always was. The loss of friends and comrades may fire the blood. It may lead men to risk their own lives in a desperate charge to get even. But it is a pain that does not rankle and that does not fester like a sore that will not heal. It is the tales the Canadians have to tell of sheer, depraved torture and brutality that has inflamed them to the pitch of hatred that they cherish. It has seemed as if the Germans had a particular grudge against the Canadians. And that, indeed, is known to be the case. The Germans harbored many a fond illusion before the war. They thought that Britain would not fight, first of all.

And then, when Britain did declare war, they thought they could speedily destroy her "contemptible little army." Ah, weel – they did come near to destroying it! But not until it had helped to balk them of their desire – not until it had played its great and decisive part in ruining the plans the Hun had been making and perfecting for forty-four long years. And not until it had served as a dyke behind which floods of men in the khaki of King George had had time to arm and drill to rush out to oppose the gray-green floods that had swept through helpless Belgium.

They had other illusions, beside that major one that helped to wreck them. They thought there would be a rebellion and civil war in Ireland. They took too seriously the troubles of the early summer of 1914, when Ulster and the South of Ireland were snapping and snarling at each other's throats. They looked for a new mutiny in India, which should keep Britain's hands full. They expected strikes at home. But, above all, they were sure that the great, self-governing dependencies of Britain, that made up the mighty British Empire, would take no part in the fight.

Canada, Australasia, South Africa – they never reckoned upon having to cope with them. These were separate nations, they thought, independent in fact if not in name, which would seize the occasion to separate themselves entirely from the mother country. In South Africa they were sure that there would be smoldering discontent enough left from the days of the Boer war to break out into a new flame of war and rebellion at this great chance.

And so it drove them mad with fury when they learned that Canada and all the rest had gone in, heart and soul. And when even their poison gas could not make the Canadians yield; when, later still, they learned that the Canadians were their match, and more than their match, in every phase of the great game of war, their rage led them to excesses against the men from overseas even more damnable than those that were their general practice.

These Canadians, who were now my hosts, had located their guns in a pit triangular in shape. The guns were mounted at the corners of the triangle, and along its sides. And constantly, while I was there they coughed their short, sharp coughs and sent a spume of metal flying toward the German lines. Never have I seen a busier spot. And, remember – until I had almost fallen into that pit, with its sputtering, busy guns, I had not been able to make even a good guess as to where they were! The very presence of this workshop of death was hidden from all save those who had a right to know of it.

It was a masterly piece of camouflage. I wish I could explain to you how the effect was achieved. It was all made plain to me; every step of the process was explained, and I cried out in wonder and in admiration at the clever simplicity of it. But that is one of the things I may not tell. I saw many things, during my time at the front, that the Germans would give a pretty penny to know. But none of the secrets that I learned would be more valuable, even to-day, than that of that hidden battery. And so – I must leave you in ignorance as to that.

The commanding officer was most kindly and patient in explaining matters to me.

"We can't see hide nor hair of our targets here, of course," he said, "any more than Fritz can see us. We get all our ranges and the records of all our hits, from Normabell."

I looked a question, I suppose.

"You called on him, I think – up on the Pimple. Major Normabell, D.S.O."

That was how I learned the name of the imperturbable major with whom I had smoked a pipe on the crest of Vimy Ridge. I shall always remember his name and him. I saw no man in France who made a livelier impression upon my mind and my imagination.

"Aye," I said. "I remember. So that's his name – Normabell, D.S.O. I'll make a note of that."

My informant smiled.

"Normabell's one of our characters," he said. "Well, you see he commands a goodish bit of country there where he sits. And when he needs them he has aircraft observations to help him, too. He's our pair of eyes.

We're like moles down here, we gunners – but he does all our seeing for us. And he's in constant communication – he or one of his officers."

I wondered where all the shells the battery was firing were headed for. And I learned that just then it was paying its respects particularly to a big factory building just west of Lens. For some reason that had been marked for destruction, but it had been reinforced and strengthened so that it was taking a lot of smashing and standing a good deal more punishment than anyone had thought it could – which was reason enough, in itself, to stick to the job until that factory was nothing more than a heap of dust and ruins.

The way the guns kept pounding away at it made me think of firemen in a small town drenching a local blaze with their hose. The gunners were just so eager as that. And I could almost see that factory, crumbling away. Major Normabell had pointed it out to me, up on the ridge, and now I knew why. I'll venture to say that before night the eight-inch howitzers of that battery had utterly demolished it, and so ended whatever usefulness it had had for the Germans.

It was cruel business to be knocking the towns and factories of our ally, France, to bits in the fashion that we were doing that day – there and at many another point along the front. The Huns are fond of saying that much of the destruction in Northern France has been the work of allied artillery. True enough – but who made that inevitable And it was not our guns that laid waste a whole countryside before the German retreat in the spring of 1917, when the Huns ran wild, rooting up fruit trees, cutting down every other tree that could be found, and doing every other sort of wanton damage and mischief their hands could find to do.

"Hard lines," said the battery commander. He shrugged his shoulders. "No use trying to spare shells here, though, even on French towns. The harder we smash them the sooner it'll be over. Look here, sir."

He pointed out the men who sat, their telephone receivers strapped over their ears. Each served a gun. In all that hideous din it was of the utmost importance that they should hear correctly every word and figure that came to them over the wire – a part of that marvelously complete telephone and telegraph system that has been built for and by the British army in France.

"They get corrections on every shot," he told me. "The guns are altered in elevation according to what they hear. The range is changed, and the pointing, too. We never see old Fritz – but we know he's getting the visiting cards we send him."

They were amazingly calm, those laddies at the telephones. In all that hideous, never-ending din, they never grew excited. Their voices were calm and steady as they repeated the orders that came to them. I have seen girls at hotel switchboards, expert operators, working with conditions made to their order, who grew infinitely more excited at a busy time, when many calls were coming in and going out. Those men might have been at home, talking to a friend of their plans for an evening's diversion, for all the nervousness or fussiness they showed.

Up there, on the Pimple, I had seen Normabell, the eyes of the battery. Here I was watching its ears. And, to finish the metaphor, to work it out, I was listening to its voice. Its brazen tongues were giving voice continually. The guns – after all, everything else led up to them. They were the reason for all the rest of the machinery of the battery, and it was they who said the last short word.

There was a good deal of rough joking and laughter in the battery. The Canadian gunners took their task lightly enough, though their work was of the hardest – and of the most dangerous, too. But jokes ran from group to group, from gun to gun. They were constantly kidding one another, as an American would say, I think. If a correction came for one gun that showed there had been a mistake in sighting after the last orders – if, that is, the gunners, and not the distant observers, were plainly at fault – there would be a good-natured outburst of chaffing from all the others.

But, though such a spirit of lightness prevailed, there was not a moment of loafing. These men were engaged in a grim, deadly task, and every once in a while I would catch a black, purposeful look in a man's eyes that made me realize that, under all the light talk and laughter there was a perfect realization of the truth. They might not show, on the surface, that they took life and their work seriously. Ah, no! They preferred, after the custom of their race, to joke with death.

And so they were doing quite literally. The Germans knew perfectly well that there was a battery somewhere near the spot where I had found my gunners. Only the exact location was hidden from them, and they never ceased their efforts to determine that. Fritz's airplanes were always trying to sneak over to get a look. An airplane was the only means of detection the Canadians feared. No – I will not say they feared it! The word fear did not exist for that battery! But it was the only way in which there was a tolerable chance, even, for Fritz to locate them, and, for the sake of the whole operation at that point, as well as for their own interest, they were eager to avoid that.

German airplanes were always trying to sneak over, I say, but nearly always our men of the Royal Flying Corps drove them back. We came as close, just then, to having command of the air in that sector as any army does these days. You cannot quite command or control the air. A few hostile flyers can get through the heaviest barrage and the staunchest air patrol. And so, every once in a while, an alarm would sound, and all hands would crane their necks upward to watch an airplane flying above with an iron cross painted upon its wings.

Then, and, as a rule, then only, fire would cease for a few minutes. There was far less chance of detection when the guns were still. At the height at which our archies – so the anti-aircraft guns are called by Tommy Atkins – forced the Boche to fly there was little chance of his observers picking out this battery, at least, against the ground. If the guns were giving voice that chance was tripled – and so they stopped, at such times, until a British flyer had had time to engage the Hun and either bring him down or send him scurrying for the safe shelter behind his own lines.

Fritz, in the air, liked to have the odds with him, as a rule. It was exceptional to find a German flyer like Boelke who really went in for single-handed duels in the air. As a rule they preferred to attack a single plane with half a dozen, and so make as sure as they could of victory at a minimum of risk. But that policy did not always work – sometimes the lone British flyer came out ahead, despite the odds against him.

There was a good deal of firing on general principles from Fritz. His shells came wandering querulously about, striking on every side of the battery. Occasionally, of course, there was a hit that was direct, or nearly so. And then, as a rule, a new mound or two would appear in the little cemetery, and a new set of crosses that, for a few days, you might easily enough have marked for new because they would not be weathered yet. But such hits were few and far between, and they were lucky, casual shots, of which the Germans themselves did not have the satisfaction of knowing.

"Of course, if they get our range, really, and find out all about us, we'll have to move," said the officer in command. "That would be a bore, but it couldn't be helped. We're a fixed target, you see, as soon as they know just where we are, and they can turn loose a battery of heavy howitzers against us and clear us out of here in no time. But we're pretty quick movers when we have to move! It's great sport, in a way too, sometimes. We leave all the camouflage behind, and sometimes Fritz will spend a week shelling a position that was moved away at the first shell that came as if it meant they really were on to us."

I wondered how a battery commander would determine the difference between a casual hit and the first shell of a bombardment definitely planned and accurately placed.

"You can tell, as a rule, if you know the game," he said. "There'll be searching shells, you see. There'll be one too far, perhaps. And then, after a pretty exact interval, there'll be another, maybe a bit short. Then one to the left – and then to the right. By that time we're off as a rule – we don't wait for the one that will be scored a hit! If you're quick, you see, you can beat Fritz to it by keeping your eyes open, and being ready to move in a hurry when he's got a really good argument to make you do it."

But while I was there, while Fritz was inquisitive enough, his curiosity got him nowhere. There were no casual hits, even, and there was nothing to make the battery feel that it must be making ready for a quick trek.

Was that no a weird, strange game of hide and seek that I watched being played at Vimy Ridge? It gave me the creeps, that idea of battling with an enemy you could not see! It must be hard, at times, I think, for, the gunners to realize that they are actually at war. But, no – there is always the drone and the squawking of the German shells, and the plop-plop, from time to time, as one finds its mark in the mud nearby. But to think of shooting always at an enemy you cannot see!

It brought to my mind a tale I had heard at hame in Scotland. There was a hospital in Glasgow, and there a man who had gone to see a friend stopped, suddenly, in amazement, at the side of a cot. He looked down at features that were familiar to him. The man in the cot was not looking at him, and the visitor stood gaping, staring at him in the utmost astonishment and doubt.

"I say, man," he asked, at last, "are ye not Tamson, the baker?"

The wounded man opened his eyes, and looked up, weakly.

"Aye," he said. "I'm Tamson, the baker." His voice was weak, and he looked tired. But he looked puzzled, too.

"Weel, Tamson, man, what's the matter wi' ye?" asked the other. "I didna hear that ye were sick or hurt. How comes it ye are here? Can it be that ye ha' been to the war, man, and we not hearing of it, at all?"

"Aye, I think so," said Tamson, still weakly, but as if he were rather glad of a chance to talk, at that.

"Ye think so?" asked his friend, in greater astonishment than ever. "Man, if ye've been to the war do ye not know it for sure and certain?"

"Well, I will tell ye how it is," said Tamson, very slowly and wearily. "I was in the reserve, do ye ken. And I was standin' in front of my hoose one day in August, thinkin' of nothin' at all. I marked a man who was coming doon the street, wi' a blue paper in his hand, and studyin' the numbers on the doorplates. But I paid no great heed to him until he stopped and spoke to me.

"He had stopped outside my hoose and looked at the number, and then at his blue paper. And then he turned to me.

"'Are ye Tamson, the baker?' he asked me – just as ye asked me that same question the noo.

"And I said to him, just as I said it to ye, 'Aye, I'm Tamson, the baker.'"

"'Then it's Hamilton Barracks for ye, Tamson,' he said, and handed me the blue paper.

"Four hours from the time when he handed me the blue paper in front of my hoose in Glasgow I was at Hamilton Barracks. In twelve hours I was in Southhampton. In twenty hours I was in France. And aboot as soon as I got there I was in a lot of shooting and running this way and that that they ha' told me since was the Battle of the Marne.

"And in twenty-four hours more I was on my way back to Glasgow! In forty-eight hours I woke up in Stobe Hill Infirmary and the nurse was saying in my ear: 'Ye're all richt the noon, Tamson. We ha' only just amputated your leg!'

"So I think I ha' been to the war, but I can only say I think so. I only know what I was told – that ha' never seen a damn German yet!"

That is a true story of Tamson the baker. And his experience has actually been shared by many a poor fellow – and by many another who might have counted himself lucky if he had lost no more than a leg, as Tamson did.

But the laddies of my battery, though they were shooting now at Germans they could not see, had had many a close up view of Fritz in the past, and expected many another in the future. Maybe they will get one, some time, after the fashion of the company of which my boy John once told me.

The captain of this company – a Hieland company, it was, though not of John's regiment – had spent must of his time in London before the war, and belonged to several clubs, which, in those days, employed many Germans as servants and waiters. He was a big man, and he had a deep, bass voice, so that he roared like the bull of Bashan when he had a mind to raise it for all to hear.

One day things were dull in his sector. The front line trench was not far from that of the Germans, but there was no activity beyond that of the snipers, and the Germans were being so cautious that ours were getting mighty few shots. The captain was bored, and so were the men.

"How would you like a pot shot, lads?" he asked.

"Fine!" came the answer. "Fine, sir!"

"Very well," said the captain. "Get ready with your rifles, and keep your eyes on you trench."

It was not more than thirty yards away – pointblank range. The captain waited until they were ready. And then his voice rang out in its loudest, most commanding roar.

"Waiter!" he shouted.

Forty helmets popped up over the German parapet, and a storm of bullets swept them away!

CHAPTER XVII

It was getting late – for men who had had so early a breakfast as we had had to make to get started in good time. And just as I was beginning to feel hungry – odd, it seemed to me, that such a thing as lunch should stay in my mind in such surroundings and when so many vastly more important things were afoot! – the major looked at his wrist watch.

"By Jove!" he said, "Lunch time! Gentlemen – you'll accept such hospitality as we can offer you at our officer's mess?"

There wasn't any question about acceptance! We all said we were delighted, and we meant it. I looked around for a hut or some such place, or even for a tent, and, seeing nothing of the sort, wondered where we might be going to eat. I soon found out. The major led the way underground, into a dugout. This was the mess. It was hard by the guns, and in a hole that had been dug out, quite literally. Here there was a certain degree of safety. In these dugouts every phase of the battery's life except the actual serving of the guns went on. Officers and men alike ate and slept in them.

They were much snugger within than you might fancy. A lot of the men had given homelike touches to their habitations. Pictures cut from the illustrated papers at home, which are such prime favorites with all the Tommies made up a large part of the decorative scheme. Pictures of actresses predominated; the Tommies didn't go in for war pictures. Indeed, there is little disposition to hammer the war home at you in a dugout. The men don't talk about it or think about, save as they must; you hear less talk about the war along the front than you do at home. I heard a story at Vimy Ridge of a Tommy who had come back to the trenches after seeing Blighty for the first time in months.

"Hello, Bill," said one of his mates. "Back again, are you? How's things in Blighty?"

"Oh, all right," said Bill.

Then he looked around. He pricked his ears as a shell whined above him. And he took out his pipe and stuffed it full of tobacco, and lighted it, and sat back. He sighed in the deepest content as the smoke began to curl upward.

"Bli'me, Bill – I'd say, to look at you, you was glad to be back here!" said his mate, astonished.

"Well, I ain't so sorry, and that's a fact," said Bill. "I tell you how it is, Alf. Back there in Blighty they don't talk about nothing but this bloody war. I'm fair fed up with it, that I am! I'm glad to be back here, where I don't have to 'ear about the war every bleedin' minute!"

That story sounds far fetched to you, perhaps, but it isn't. War talk is shop talk to the men who are fighting it and winning it, and it is perfectly true and perfectly reasonable, too, that they like to get away from it when they can, just as any man likes to get away from the thought of his business or his work when he isn't at the office or the factory or the shop.

Captain Godfrey explained to me, as we went into the mess hall for lunch, that the dugouts were really pretty safe. Of course there were dangers – where are there not along that strip of land that runs from the North Sea to Switzerland in France and Belgium?

"A direct hit from a big enough shell would bury us all," he said. "But that's not likely – the chances are all against it. And, even then, we'd have a chance. I've seen men dug out alive from a hole like this after a shell from one of their biggest howitzers had landed square upon it."

But I had no anxiety to form part of an experiment to prove the truth or the falsity of that suggestion! I was glad to know that the chances of a shell's coming along were pretty slim.

Conditions were primitive at that mess. The refinements of life were lacking, to be sure – but who cared? Certainly the hungry members of the Reverend Harry Lauder, M.P., Tour did not! We ate from a rough deal table, sitting on rude benches that had a decidedly homemade look. But – we had music with our meals, just like the folks in London at the Savoy or in New York at Sherry's! It was the incessant thunder of the guns that served as the musical accompaniment of our lunch, and I was already growing to love that music. I could begin, now, to distinguish degrees of sound and modulations of all sorts in the mighty diapason of the cannon. It was as if a conductor were leading an orchestra, and as if it responded instantly to every suggestion of his baton.

There was not much variety to the food, but there was plenty of it, and it was good. There was bully beef, of course; that is the real staff of life for the British army. And there were potatoes, in plentiful supply, and bread and butter, and tea – there is always tea where Tommy or his officers are about! There was a lack of table ware; a dainty soul might not have liked the thought of spreading his butter on his bread with his thumb, as we had to do. But I was too hungry to be fastidious, myself.

Because the mess had guests there was a special dish in our honor. One of the men had gone over – at considerable risk of his life, as I learned later – to the heap of stones and dust that had once been the village of Givenchy. There he had found a lot of gooseberries. The French call them grossets, as we in Scotland do, too – although the pronunciation of the word is different in the two languages, of course. There had been gardens around the houses of Givenchy once, before the place had been made into a desert of rubble and brickdust. And, somehow, life had survived in those bruised and battered gardens, and the delicious mess of gooseberries that we had for dessert stood as proof thereof.

The meal was seasoned by good talk. I love to hear the young British officers talk. It is a liberal education. They have grown so wise, those boys! Those of them who come back when the war is over will have the world at their feet, indeed. Nothing will be able to stop them or to check them in their rise. They have learned every great lesson that a man must learn if he is to succeed in the affairs of life. Self control is theirs, and an infinite patience, and a dogged determination that refuses to admit that there are any things that a man cannot do if he only makes up his mind that he must and will do them. For the British army has accomplished the impossible, time after time; it has done things that men knew could not be done.

And so we sat and talked, as we smoked, after the meal, until the major rose, at last, and invited me to walk around the battery again with him. I could ask questions now, having seen the men at work, and he explained many things I wanted to know – and which Fritz would like to know, too, to this day! But above all I was fascinated by the work of the gunners. I kept trying, in my mind's eye, to follow the course of the shells that were dispatched so calmly upon their errands of destruction. My imagination played with the thought of what they were doing at the other end of their swift voyage through the air. I pictured the havoc that must be wrought when one made a clean hit.

And, suddenly, I was swept by that same almost irresistible desire to be fighting myself that had come over me when I had seen the other battery. If I could only play my part! If I could fire even a single shot – if I, with my own hands, could do that much against those who had killed my boy! And then, incredulously, I heard the words in my ear. It was the major.

"Would you like to try a shot, Harry?" he asked me.

Would I? I stared at him. I couldn't believe my ears. It was as if he had read my thoughts. I gasped out some sort of an affirmative. My blood was boiling at the very thought, and the sweat started from my pores.

"All right – nothing easier!" said the major, smiling. "I had an idea you were wanting to take a hand, Harry."

He led me toward one of the guns, where the sweating crew was especially active, as it seemed to me. They grinned at me as they saw me coming.

"Here's old Harry Lauder come to take a crack at them himself," I heard one man say to another.

"Good for him! The more the merrier!" answered his mate. He was an American – would ye no know it from his speech?

I was trembling with eagerness. I wondered if my shot would tell. I tried to visualize its consequences. It might strike some vital spot. It might kill some man whose life was of the utmost value to the enemy. It might – it might do anything! And I knew that my shot would be watched; Normabell, sitting up there on the Pimple in his little observatory, would watch it, as he did all of that battery's shots. Would he make a report?

Everything was made ready. The gun recoiled from the previous shot; swiftly it was swabbed out. A new shell was handed up; I looked it over tenderly. That was my shell! I watched the men as they placed it and saw it disappear with a jerk. Then came the swift sighting of the gun, the almost imperceptible corrections of elevation and position.

They showed me my place. After all, it was the simplest of matters to fire even the biggest of guns. I had but to pull a lever. All morning I had been watching men do that. I knew it was but a perfunctory act. But I could not feel that! I was thrilled and excited as I had never been in all my life before.

"All ready! Fire!"

The order rang in my ears. And I pulled the lever, as hard as I could. The great gun sprang into life as I moved the lever. I heard the roar of the explosion, and it seemed to me that it was a louder bark than any gun I had heard had given! It was not, of course, and so, down in my heart, I knew. There was no shade of variation between that shot and all the others that had been fired. But it pleased me to think so – it pleases me, sometimes, to think so even now. Just as it pleases me to think that that long snouted engine of war propelled that shell, under my guiding hand, with unwonted accuracy and effectiveness! Perhaps I was childish, to feel as I did; indeed, I have no doubt that that was so. But I dinna care!

There was no report by telephone from Normabell about that particular shot; I hung about a while, by the telephone listeners, hoping one would come. And it disappointed me that no attention was paid to that shot.

"Probably simply means it went home," said Godfrey. "A shot that acts just as it should doesn't get reported."

But I was disappointed, just the same. And yet the sensation is one I shall never forget, and I shall never cease to be glad that the major gave me my chance. The most thrilling moment was that of the recoil of the great gun. I felt exactly as one does when one dives into deep water from a considerable height.

"Good work, Harry!" said the major, warmly, when I had stepped down. "I'll wager you wiped out a bit of the German trenches with that shot! I think I'll draft you and keep you here as a gunner!"

And the officers and men all spoke in the same way, smiling as they did so. But I hae me doots! I'd like to think I did real damage with my one shot, but I'm afraid my shell was just one of those that turned up a bit of dirt and made one of those small brown eruptions I had seen rising on all sides along the German lines as I had sat and smoked my pipe with Normabell earlier in the day.

"Well, anyway," I said, exultingly, "that's that! I hope I got two for my one, at least!"

But my exultation did not last long. I reflected upon the inscrutability of war and of this deadly fighting that was going on all about me. How casual a matter was this sending out of a shell that could, in a flash of time, obliterate all that lived in a wide circle about where it chanced to strike! The pulling of a lever – that was all that I had done! And at any moment a shell some German gunner had sent winging its way through the air in precisely that same, casual fashion might come tearing into this quiet nook, guided by some chance, lucky for him, and wipe out the major, and all the pleasant boys with whom I had broken bread just now, and the sweating gunners who had cheered me on as I fired my shot!

I was to give a concert for this battery, and I felt that it was time, now, for it to begin. I could see, too, that the men were growing a bit impatient. And so I said that I was ready.

"Then come along to our theater," said the major, and grinned at my look of astonishment.

"Oh, we've got a real amphitheater for you, such as the Greeks used for the tragedies of Sophocles!" he said. "There it is!"

He had not stretched the truth. It was a superb theater – a great, crater-like hole in the ground. Certainly it was as well ventilated a show house as you could hope for, and I found, when the time came, that the acoustics were splendid. I went down into the middle of the hole, with Hogge and Adam, who had become part of my company, and the soldiers grouped themselves about its rim.

Before we left Boulogne a definite programme had been laid out for the Reverend Harry Lauder, M.P., Tour. We had decided that we would get better results by adopting a programme and sticking to it at all our meetings or concerts. So, at all the assemblies that we gathered, Hogge opened proceedings by talking to the men about pensions, the subject in which he was so vitally interested, and in which he had done and was doing such magnificent work. Adam would follow him with a talk about the war and its progress.

He was a splendid speaker, was Adam. He had all the eloquence of the fine preacher that he was, but he did not preach to the lads in the trenches – not he! He told them about the war, and about the way the folks at hame in Britain were backing them up. He talked about war loans and food conservation, and made them understand that it was not they alone who were doing the fighting. It was a cheering and an inspiring talk he gave them, and he got good round applause wherever he spoke.

They saved me up for the last, and when Adam had finished speaking either he or Hogge would introduce me, and my singing would begin. That was the programme we had arranged for the Hole-in-the-Ground Theater, as the

Canadians called their amphitheater. For this performance, of course, I had no piano. Johnson and the wee instrument were back where we had left the motor cars, and so I just had to sing without an accompaniment – except that which the great booming of the guns was to furnish me.

I was afraid at first that the guns would bother me. But as I listened to Hogge and Adam I ceased, gradually, to notice them at all, and I soon felt that they would annoy me no more, when it was my turn to go on, than the chatter of a bunch of stage hands in the wings of a theater had so often done.

When it was my turn I began with "Roamin' in the Gloamin'." The verse went well, and I swung into the chorus. I had picked the song to open with because I knew the soldiers were pretty sure to know it, and so would join me in the chorus – which is something I always want them to do. And these were no exceptions to the general rule. But, just as I got into the chorus, the tune of the guns changed. They had been coughing and spitting intermittently, but now, suddenly, it seemed to me that it was as if someone had kicked the lid off the fireworks factory and dropped a lighted torch inside.

Every gun in the battery around the hole began whanging away at once. I was jumpy and nervous, I'll admit, and it was all I could do to hold to the pitch and not break the time. I thought all of Von Hindenburg's army must be attacking us, and, from the row and din, I judged he must have brought up some of the German navy to help, instead of letting it lie in the Kiel canal where the British fleet could not get at it. I never heard such a terrific racket in all my days.

I took the opportunity to look around at my audience. They didn't seem to be a bit excited. They all had their eyes fixed on me, and they weren't listening to the guns – only to me and my singing. And so, as they probably knew what was afoot, and took it so quietly, I managed to keep on singing as if I, too, were used to such a row, and thought no more of it than of the ordinary traffic noise of a London or a Glasgow street. But if I really managed to look that way my appearances were most deceptive, because I was nearer to being scared than I had been at any time yet!

But presently I began to get interested in the noise of the guns. They developed a certain regular rhythm. I had to allow for it, and make it fit the time of what I was singing. And as I realized that probably this was just a part of the regular day's work, a bit of ordinary strafing, and not a feature of a grand attack, I took note of the rhythm. It went something like this, as near as I can gie it to you in print:

"Roamin' in the – PUH – LAH – Gloamin' – BAM! On the – WHUFF! – BOOM! – bonny – BR-R-R! – banks o' – BIFF – Clyde – ZOW!"

And so it went all through the rest of the concert. I had to adjust each song I sang to that odd rhythm of the guns, and I don't know but what it was just as well that Johnson wasn't there! He'd have had trouble staying with me with his wee bit piano, I'm thinkin'!

And, do you ken, I got to see, after a bit, that it was the gunners, all the time, havin' a bit of fun with me! For when I sang a verse the guns behaved themselves, but every time I came to the chorus they started up the same inferno of noise again. I think they wanted to see, at first, if they could no shake me enough to make me stop singing, and they liked me the better when they found I would no stop. The soldiers soon began to laugh, but the joke was not all on me, and I could see that they understood that, and were pleased. Indeed, it was all as amusing to me as to them.

I doubt if "Roamin' in the Gloamin'" or any other song was ever sung in such circumstances. I sang several more songs – they called, as every audience I have seems to do, for me to sing my "Wee Hoose Amang the Heather" – and then Captain Godfrey brought the concert to an end. It was getting along toward midafternoon, and he explained that we had another call to make before dark.

"Good-by, Harry – good luck to you! Thanks for the singing!"

Such cries rose from all sides, and the Canadians came crowding around to shake my hand. It was touching to see how pleased they were, and it made me rejoice that I had been able to come. I had thought, sometimes, that it might be a presumptuous thing, in a way, for me to want to go so near the front, but the way I had been able to cheer up the lonely, dull routine of that battery went far to justify me in coming, I thought.

I was sorry to be leaving the Canadians. And I was glad to see that they seemed as sorry to have me go as I was to be going. I have a very great fondness for the Canadian soldier. He is certainly one of the most picturesque and interesting of all the men who are fighting under the flags of the Allies, and it is certain that the world can never forget the record he has made in this war – a record of courage and heroism unexcelled by any and equaled by few.

I stood around while we were getting ready to start back to the cars, and one of the officers was with me.

"How often do you get a shell right inside the pit here?" I asked him. "A fair hit, I mean?"

"Oh, I don't know!" he said, slowly. He looked around. "You know that hole you were singing in just now?"

I nodded. I had guessed that it had been made by a shell.

"Well, that's the result of a Boche shell," he said. "If you'd come yesterday we'd have had to find another place for your concert!"

"Oh – is that so!" I said.

"Aye," he said, and grinned. "We didn't tell you before, Harry, because we didn't want you to feel nervous, or anything like that, while you were singing. But it was obliging of Fritz – now wasn't it? Think of having him take all the trouble to dig out a fine theater for us that way!"

"It was obliging of him, to be sure," I said, rather dryly.

"That's what we said," said the officer. "Why, as soon as I saw the hole that shell had made, I said to Campbell: 'By Jove – there's the very place for Harry Lauder's concert to-morrow!' And he agreed with me!"

Now it was time for handshaking and good-bys. I said farewell all around, and wished good luck to that brave battery, so cunningly hidden away in its pit. There was a great deal of cheery shouting and waving of hands as we went off. And in two minutes the battery was out of sight – even though we knew exactly where it was!

We made our way slowly back, through the lengthening shadows, over the shell-pitted ground. The motor cars were waiting, and Johnson, too. Everything was shipshape and ready for a new start, and we climbed in.

As we drove off I looked back at Vimy Ridge. And I continued to gaze at it for a long time. No longer did it disappoint me. No longer did I regard it as an insignificant hillock. All that feeling that had come to me with my first sight of it had been banished by my introduction to the famous ridge itself.

It had spoken to me eloquently, despite the muteness of the myriad tongues it had. It had graven deep into my heart the realization of its true place in history.

An excrescence in a flat country – a little hump of ground! That is all there is to Vimy Ridge. Aye! It does not stand so high above the ground of Flanders as would the books that will be written about it in the future, were you to pile them all up together when the last one of them is printed! But what a monument it is to bravery and to sacrifice – to all that is best in this human race of ours!

No human hands have ever reared such a monument as that ridge is and will be. There some of the greatest deeds in history were done – some of the noblest acts that there is record of performed. There men lived and died gloriously in their brief moment of climax – the moment for which, all unknowing, all their lives before that day of battle had been lived.

I took off my cap as I looked back, with a gesture and a thought of deep and solemn reverence. And so I said good-by to Vimy Ridge, and to the brave men I had known there – living and dead. For I felt that I had come to know some of the dead as well as the living.

CHAPTER XVIII

"You'll see another phase of the front now, Harry," said Captain Godfrey, as I turned my eyes to the front once more.

"What's the next stop?" I asked.

"We're heading for a rest billet behind the lines. There'll be lots of men there who are just out of the trenches. It's a ghastly strain for even the best and most seasoned troops – this work in the trenches. So, after a battalion has been in for a certain length of time, it's pulled out and sent back to a rest billet."

"What do they do there?" I asked.

"Well, they don't loaf – there's none of that in the British army, these days! But it's paradise, after the trenches. For one thing there isn't the constant danger there is up front. The men aren't under steady fire. Of course, there's always the chance of a bomb dropping raid by a Taube or a Fokker. The men get a chance to clean up.

They get baths, and their clothes are cleaned and disinfected. They get rid of the cooties – you know what they are?"

I could guess. The plague of vermin in the trenches is one of the minor horrors of war.

"They do a lot of drilling," Godfrey went on. "Except for those times in the rest billets, regiments might get a bit slack. In the trenches, you see, the routine is strict, but it's different. Men are much more on their own. There aren't any inspections of kit and all that sort of thing – not for neatness, anyway.

"And it's a good thing for soldiers to be neat. It helps discipline. And discipline, in time of war, isn't just a parade-ground matter. It means lives – every time. Your disciplined man, who's trained to do certain things automatically, is the man you can depend on in any sort of emergency.

"That's the thing that the Canadians and the Australians have had to learn since they came out. There never were any braver troops than those in the world, but at first they didn't have the automatic discipline they needed. That'll be the first problem in training the new American armies, too. It's a highly practical matter. And so, in the rest billets, they drill the men a goodish bit. It keeps up the morale, and makes them fitter and keener for the work when they go back to the trenches."

"You don't make it sound much like a real rest for them," I said.

"Oh, but it is, all right! They have a comfortable place to sleep. They get better food. The men in the trenches get the best food it's possible to give them, but it can't be cooked much, for there aren't facilities. The diet gets pretty monotonous. In the rest billets they get more variety. And they have plenty of free time, and there are hours when they can go to the estaminet – there's always one handy, a sort of pub, you know – and buy things for themselves. Oh, they have a pretty good time, as you'll see, in a rest billet."

I had to take his word for it. We went bowling along at a good speed, but pretty soon we encountered a detachment of Somerset men. They halted when they spied our caravan, and so did we. As usual they recognized us.

"You'm Harry Lauder!" said one of them, in the broad accent of his country. "Us has seen 'ee often!"

Johnson was out already, and he and the drivers were unlimbering the wee piano. It didn't take so long, now that we were getting used to the task, to make ready for a roadside concert. While I waited I talked to the men. They were on their way to Ypres. Tommy can't get the name right, and long ago ceased trying to do so. The French and Belgians call it "Eepre" – that's as near as I can give it to you in print, at least. But Tommy, as all the world must know by now, calls it Wipers, and that is another name that will live as long as British history is told.

The Somerset men squatted in the road while I sang my songs for them, and gave me their most rapt attention. It was hugely gratifying and flattering, the silence that always descended upon an audience of soldiers when I sang. There were never any interruptions. But at the end of a song, and during the chorus, which they always wanted to sing with me, as I wanted them to do, too, they made up for their silence.

Soon the Reverend Harry Lauder, M.P., Tour was on its way again. The cheers of the Somerset men sounded gayly in our ears, and the cars quickly picked up speed and began to mop up the miles at a great rate. And then, suddenly –whoa! We were in the midst of soldiers again. This time it was a bunch of motor repair men.

They wandered along the roads, working on the trucks and cars that were abandoned when they got into trouble, and left along the side of the road. We had seen scores of such wrecks that day, and I had wondered if they were left there indefinitely. Far from it, as I learned now. Squads like this – there were two hundred men in this particular party – were always at work. Many of the cars they salvaged without difficulty – those that had been abandoned because of comparatively minor engine troubles or defects. Others had to be towed to a repair shop, or loaded upon other trucks for the journey, if their wheels were out of commission.

Others still were beyond repair. They had been utterly smashed in a collision, maybe, or as a result of skidding. Or they had burned. Sometimes they had been knocked off the road and generally demoralized by a shell. And in such cases often, all that men such as these we had met now could do was to retrieve some parts to be used in repairing other cars in a less hopeless state.

By this time Johnson and the two soldier chauffeurs had reduced the business of setting our stage to a fine point. It took us but a very few minutes indeed to be ready for a concert, and from the time when we sighted a potential audience to the moment for the opening number was an almost incredibly brief period. This time that was a good thing, for it was growing late. And so, although the repair men were loath to let me go, it was but an abbreviated programme that I was able to offer them. This was one of the most enthusiastic audiences I had had yet, for nearly every man there, it turned out, had been what Americans would call a Harry Lauder fan in the old days. They had been wont to go again and again to hear me. I wanted to stay and sing more songs for them, but Captain Godfrey was in charge, and I had to obey his orders, reluctant though I was to go on.

Our destination was a town called Aubigny – rather an old château just outside the town. Aubigny was the billet of the Fifteenth Division, then in rest. Many officers were quartered in the château, as the guests of its French owners, who remained in possession, having refused to clear out, despite the nearness of the actual fighting front.

This was a Scots division, I was glad to find. I heard good Scots talk all around me when I arrived, and it was Scottish hospitality, mingled with French, that awaited us. I know no finer combination, nor one more warming to the cockles of a man's heart.

Here there was luxury, compared to what I had seen that day. As Godfrey had warned me, the idea of resting that the troops had was a bit more strenuous than mine would be. There was no lying and lolling about. Hot though the weather was a deal of football was played, and there were games of one sort and another going on nearly all the time when the men were off duty.

This division, I learned, had seen some of the hardest and bloodiest fighting of the whole war. They had been through the great offensive that had pivoted on Arras, and had been sorely knocked about. They had well earned such rest as was coming to them now, and they were getting ready, in the most cheerful way you can imagine, for their next tour of duty in the trenches. They knew about how much time they would have, and they made the best use they could of it.

New drafts were coming out daily from home to fill up their sadly depleted ranks. The new men were quickly drawn in and assimilated into organizations that had been reduced to mere skeletons. New officers were getting acquainted with their men; that wonderful thing that is called esprit de corps was being made all around me. It is a great sight to watch it in the making; it helps you to understand the victories our laddies have won.

I was glad to see the kilted men of the Scots regiments all about me. It was them, after all, that I had come to see. I wanted to talk to them, and see them here, in France. I had seen them at hame, flocking to the recruiting offices. I had seen them in their training camps. But this was different. I love all the soldiers of the Empire, but it is natural, is it no, that my warmest feeling should be for the laddies who wear the kilt.

They were the most cheerful souls, as I saw them when we reached their rest camp, that you could imagine. They were laughing and joking all about us, and when they heard that the Reverend Harry Lauder, M.P., Tour had arrived they crowded about us to see. They wanted to make sure that I was there, and I was greeted in all sorts of dialect that sounded enough, I'll be bound, to Godfrey and some of the rest of our party. There were even men who spoke to me in the Gaelic.

I saw a good deal, afterward, of these Scots troops. My, how hard they did work while they rested! And what chances they took of broken bones and bruises in their play! Ye would think, would ye no, that they had enough of that in the trenches, where they got lumps and bruises and sorer hurts in the run of duty? But no. So soon as they came back to their rest billets they must begin to play by knocking the skin and the hair off one another at sports of various sorts, of which football was among the mildest, that are not by any means to be recommended to those of a delicate fiber.

Some of the men I met at Aubigny had been out since Mons – some of the old kilted regiments of the old regular army, they were. Away back in those desperate days the Germans had dubbed them the Ladies from Hell, on account of their kilts. Some of the Germans really thought they were women! That was learned from prisoners. Since Mons they have been out, and auld Scotland has poured out men by the scores of thousands, as fast as they were needed, to fill the gaps the German shells and bullets have torn in the Scots ranks. Aye – since Mons, and they will be there at the finish, when it comes, please God!

There have always been Scots regiments in the British army, ever since the day when King Jamie the Sixth, of Scotland, of the famous and unhappy house of Stuart, became King James the First of England. The kilted regiments, the Highlanders, belonging to the immortal Highland Brigade, include the Gordon Highlanders, the Forty-second, the world famous Black Watch, as it is better known than by its numbered designation, the

Seaforth Highlanders, and the Argyle and Sutherland regiment, or the Princess Louise's Own. That was the regiment to a territorial battalion of which my boy John belonged at the outbreak of the war, and with which he served until he was killed.

Some of those old, famous regiments have been wiped out half a dozen times, almost literally annihilated, since Mons. New drafts, and the addition of territorial battalions, have replenished them and kept up their strength, and the continuity of their tradition has never been broken. The men who compose a regiment may be wiped out, but the regiment survives. It is an organization, an entity, a creature with a soul as well as a body. And the Germans have no discovered a way yet of killing the soul! They can do dreadful things to the bodies of men and women, but their souls are safe from them.

Of course there are Scots regiments that are not kilted and that have naught to do with the Hielanders, who have given as fine and brave an account of themselves as any. There are the Scots Guards, one of the regiments of the Guards Brigade, the very pick and flower of the British army. There are the King's Own Scottish Borderers, with as fine a history and tradition as any regiment in the army, and a record of service of which any regiment might well be proud; the Scots Fusiliers, the Royal Scots, the Scottish Rifles, and the Scots Greys, of Crimean fame – the only cavalry regiment from Scotland.

Since this war began other Highland regiments have been raised beside those originally included in the Highland Brigade. There are Scots from Canada who wear the kilt and their own tartan and cap. Every Highland regiment, of course, has its own distinguishing tartan and cap. One of the proudest moments of my life came when I heard that the ninth battalion of the Highland Light Infantry, which was raised in Glasgow, but has its depot, where its recruits and new drafts are trained, at Hamilton, was known as the Harry Lauders. That was because they had adopted the Balmoral cap, with dice, that had become associated with me because I had worn it so often and so long on the stage in singing one of my most famous and successful songs, "I Love a Lassie."

But in the trenches, of course, the Hieland troops all look alike. They cling to their kilts – or, rather, their kilts cling to them – but kilts and jackets are all of khaki. If they wore the bright plaids of the tartans they would be much too conspicuous a mark for the Germans, and so they have to forswear their much loved colors when they are actually at grips with Fritz.

I wear the kilt nearly always, myself, as I have said. Partly I do so because it is my native costume, and I am proud of my Highland birth; partly because I revel in the comfort of the costume. But it brings me some amusing experiences. Very often I am asked a question that is, I presume, fired at many a Hieland soldier, intimate though it is.

"I say, Harry," someone will ask me, "you wear the kilt. Do you not wear anything underneath it?"

I do, myself. I wear a very short pair of trunks, chiefly for reasons of modesty. So do some of the soldiers. But if they do they must provide it for themselves; no such garment is served out to them with their uniform. And so the vast majority of the men wear nothing but their skins under the kilt. He is bare, that is, from the waist to the hose – except for the kilt. But that is garment enough! I'll tell ye so, and I'm thinkin' I know!

So clad the Highland soldier is a great deal more comfortable and a great deal more sanely dressed, I believe, than the city dweller who is trousered and underweared within an inch of his life. I think it is a matter of medical record, that can be verified from the reports of the army surgeons, that the kilted troops are among the healthiest in the whole army. I know that the Highland troops are much less subject to abdominal troubles of all sorts – colic and the like. The kilt lies snug and warm around the stomach, in several thick layers, and a more perfect protection from the cold has never been devised for that highly delicate and susceptible region of the human anatomy.

Women, particularly, are always asking me another question. I have seen them eyeing me, in cold weather, when I was walkin' around, comfortably, in my kilt. And their eyes would wander to my knees, and I would know before they opened their mouths what it was that they were going to say.

"Oh, Mr. Lauder," they would ask me. "Don't your poor knees get cold – with no coverings, exposed to this bitter cold?"

Well, they never have! That's all I can tell you. They have had the chance, in all sorts of bitter weather. I am not thinking only of the comparatively mild winters of Britain – although, up north, in Scotland, we get some pretty severe winter weather. But I have been in Western Canada, and in the northwestern states of the United

States, Montana, North Dakota, Minnesota, where the thermometer drops far below zero. And my knees have never been cold yet. They do not suffer from the cold any more than does my face, which is as little covered and protected as they – and for the same reason, I suppose. They are used to the weather.

And when it comes to the general question of health, I am certain, from my own experience, that the kilt is best. Several times, for one reason or another, I have laid my kilts aside and put on trousers. And each time I have been seized by violent colds, and my life has been made wretched. A good many soldiers of my acquaintance have had the same experience.

Practical reasons aside, however, the Scots soldier loves his kilt, and would fight like a steer to keep from having it taken away from him, should anyone be so foolish as to try such a performance. He loves it, not only because it is warm and comfortable, but because it is indistinguishably associated in his mind with some of the most glorious pages of Scottish history. It is a sign and symbol of his hameland to him. There have been times, in Scotland, when all was not as peaceful in the country's relations with England as it now is, when the loyal Scot who wore the kilt did so knowing that he might be tried for his life for doing so, since death had been the penalty appointed for that "crime."

Aye, it is peace and friendship now between Scot and Englishman. But that is not to say that there is no a friendly rivalry between them still. English regiments and Scots regiments have a lot of fun with one another, and a bit rough it gets, too, at times. But it is all in fun, and there is no harm done. I have in mind a tale an officer told me – though the men of whom he told it did not know that an officer had any inkling of the story.

The English soldiers are very fond of harping on the old idea of the difficulty of making a Scotsman see a joke. That is a base slander, I'll say, but no matter. There were two regiments in rest close to one another, one English and one Scots. They met at the estaminet or pub in the nearby town. And one day the Englishman put up a great joke on some of the Scots, and did get a little proof of that pet idea of theirs, for the Scots were slow to see the joke.

Ah, weel, that was enough! For days the English rang the changes on that joke, teasing the Hielanders and making sport of them. But at last, when the worst of the tormentors were all assembled together, two of the Scots came into the room where they were havin' a wee drappie.

"Mon, Sandy," said one of them, shaking his head, "I've been thinking what a sad thing that would be! I hope it will no come to pass."

"Aye, that would be a sore business, indeed, Tam," said Sandy, and he, too, shook his head.

And so they went on. The Englishmen stood it as long as they could and then one turned to Sandy.

"What is it would be such a bad business?" he asked.

"Mon-mon," said Sandy. "We've been thinking, Tam and I, what would become of England, should Scotland make a separate peace?"

And it was generally conceded that the last laugh was with the Scots in that affair!

My boy, John, had the same love for the kilt that I had. He was proud and glad to wear the kilt, and to lead men who did the same. While he was in training at Bedford he organized a corps of cyclists for dispatch-bearing work. He was a crack cyclist himself, and it was a sport of which he was passionately fond. So he took a great interest in the corps, and it soon gained wide fame for its efficiency. So true was that that the authorities took note of the corps, and of John, who was responsible for it, and he was asked to go to France to take charge of organizing a similar corps behind the front. But that would have involved a transfer to a different branch of the army, and detachment from his regiment. And – it would have meant that he must doff his kilt. Since he had the chance to decline – it was an offer, not an order, that had come to him – he did, that he might keep his kilt and stay with his own men.

To my eyes there is no spectacle that begins to be so imposing as the sight of a parade of Scottish troops in full uniform. And it is the unanimous testimony of German prisoners that this war has brought them no more terrifying sight than the charge of a kilted regiment. The Highlanders come leaping forward, their bayonets gleaming, shouting old battle cries that rang through the glens years and centuries ago, and that have come down to the descendants of the warriors of an ancient time. The Highlanders love to use cold steel; the claymore was their old weapon, and the bayonet is its nearest equivalent in modern war. They are master hands with that, too – and the bayonet is the one thing the Hun has no stomach for at all.

Fritz is brave enough when he is under such cover and shelter as the trenches give. And he has shown a sort of stubborn courage when attacking in massed formations – the Germans have made terrible sacrifices, at times, in their offensive efforts. But his blood turns to water in his veins when he sees the big braw laddies from the Hielands come swooping toward him, their kilts flapping and their bayonets shining in whatever light there is. Then he is mighty quick to throw up his hands and shout: "Kamerad! Kamerad!"

I might go on all night telling you some of the stories I heard along the front about the Scottish soldiers. They illustrate and explain every phase of his character. They exploit his humor, despite that base slander to which I have already referred, his courage, his stoicism. And, of course, a vast fund of stories has sprung up that deals with the proverbial thrift of the Scot! There was one tale that will bear repeating, perhaps.

Two Highlanders had captured a chicken – a live chicken, not particularly fat, it may be, even a bit scrawny, but still, a live chicken. That was a prize, since the bird seemed to have no owner who might get them into trouble with the military police. One was for killing and eating the fowl at once. But the other would have none of such a summary plan.

"No, no, Jimmy," he said, pleadingly, holding the chicken protectingly. "Let's keep her until morning, and may be we will ha' an egg as well!"

The other British soldiers call the Scots Jock, invariably. The Englishman, or a soldier from Wales or Ireland, as a rule, is called Tommy – after the well-known M. Thomas Atkins. Sometimes, an Irishman will be Paddy and a Welshman Taffy. But the Scot is always Jock.

Jock gave us a grand welcome at Aubigny. We were all pretty tired, but when they told me I could have an audience of seven thousand Scots soldiers I forgot my weariness, and Hogge, Adam and I, to say nothing of Johnson and the wee piano, cleared for action, as you might say. The concert was given in the picturesque grounds of the château, which had been less harshly treated by the war than many such beautiful old places. It was a great experience to sing to so many men; it was far and away the largest house we had had since we had landed at Boulogne.

After we left Aubigny, the château and that great audience, we drove on as quickly as we could, since it was now late, to the headquarters of General Mac —, commanding the Fifteenth Division – to which, of course, the men whom we had just been entertaining belonged. I was to meet the general upon my arrival.

That was a strange ride. It was pitch dark, and we had some distance to go. There were mighty few lights in evidence; you do not advertise a road to Fritz's airplanes when you are traveling roads anywhere near the front, for he has guns of long range, that can at times manage to strafe a road that is supposed to be beyond the zone of fire with a good deal of effect. I have seldom seen a blacker night than that. Objects along the side of the road were nothing but shapeless lumps, and I did not see how our drivers could manage at all to find their way.

They seemed to have no difficulty, however, but got along swimmingly. Indeed, they traveled faster than they had in daylight. Perhaps that was because we were not meeting troops to hold us up along this road; I believe that, if we had, we should have stopped and given them a concert, even though Johnson could not have seen the keys of his piano!

It was just as well, however. I was delighted at the reception that had been given to the Reverend Harry Lauder, M.P., Tour all through our first day in France. But I was also extremely tired, and the dinner and bed that loomed up ahead of us, at the end of our long ride through the dark, took on an aspect of enchantment as we neared them. My voice, used as I was to doing a great deal of singing, was fagged, and Hogge and Dr. Adam were so hoarse that they could scarcely speak at all. Even Johnson was pretty well done up; he was still, theoretically, at least, on the sick list, of course. And I ha' no doot that the wee piano felt it was entitled to its rest, too!

So we were all mighty glad when the cars stopped at last.

"Well, here we are!" said Captain Godfrey, who was the freshest of us all. "This is Tramecourt – General Headquarters for the Reverend Harry Lauder, M.P., Tour while you are in France, gentlemen. They have special facilities for visitors here, and unless one of Fritz's airplanes feels disposed to drop a bomb or two, you won't be under fire, at night at least. Of course, in the daytime —."

He shrugged his shoulders. For our plans did not involve a search for safe places. Still, it was pleasant to know that we might sleep in fair comfort.

General Mac — was waiting to welcome us, and told us that dinner was ready and waiting, which we were all glad to hear. It had been a long, hard day, although the most interesting one, by far, that I had ever spent.

We made short work of dinner, and soon afterward they took us to our rooms. I don't know what Hogge and Dr. Adam did, but I know I looked happily at the comfortable bed that was in my room. And I slept easily and without being rocked to sleep that nicht!

CHAPTER XIX

Though we were out of the zone of fire – except for stray activities in which Boche airplanes might indulge themselves, as our hosts were frequently likely to remind us, lest we fancy ourselves too secure, I suppose – we were by no means out of hearing of the grim work that was going on a few miles away. The big guns, of course, are placed well behind the front line trenches, and we could hear their sullen, constant quarreling with Fritz and his artillery. The rumble of the Hun guns came to us, too. But that is a sound to which you soon get used, out there in France. You pay no more heed to it than you do to the noise the 'buses make in London or the trams in Glasgow.

In the morning I got my first chance really to see Tramecourt. The château is a lovely one, a fine example of such places. It had not been knocked about at all, and it looked much as it must have done in times of peace. Practically all the old furniture was still in the rooms, and there were some fine old pictures on the walls that it gave me great delight to see. Indeed, the rare old atmosphere of the château was restful and delightful in a way that surprised me.

I had been in the presence of real war for just one day. And yet I took pleasure in seeing again the comforts and some of the luxuries of peace! That gave me an idea of what this sort of place must mean to men from the trenches. It must seem like a bit of heaven to them to come back to Aubigny or Tramecourt! Think of the contrast.

The château, which had been taken over by the British army, belonged to the Comte de Chabot, or, rather, to his wife, who had been Marquise de Tramecourt, one of the French families of the old regimé. Although the old nobility of France has ceased to have any legal existence under the Republic the old titles are still used as a matter of courtesy, and they have a real meaning and value. This was a pleasant place, this château of Tramecourt; I should like to see it again in days of peace, for then it must be even more delightful than it was when I came to know it so well.

Tramecourt was to be our home, the headquarters of the Reverend Harry Lauder, M.P., Tour, during the rest of our stay at the front. We were to start out each morning, in the cars, to cover the ground appointed for that day, and to return at night. But it was understood that there would be days when we would get too far away to return at night, and other sleeping quarters would be provided on such occasions.

I grew very fond of the place while I was there. The steady pounding of the guns did not disturb my peace of nights, as a rule. But there was one night when I did lie awake for hours, listening. Even to my unpracticed ear there was a different quality in the sound of the cannon that night. It had a fury, an intensity, that went beyond anything I had heard. And later I learned that I had made no mistake in thinking that there was something unusual and portentous about the fire that night. What I had listened to was the preliminary drum fire and bombardment that prepared the way for the great attack at Messines, near Ypres – the most terrific bombardment recorded in all history, up to that time.

The fire that night was like a guttural chant. It had a real rhythm; the beat of the guns could almost be counted. And at dawn there came the terrific explosion of the great mine that had been prepared, which was the signal for the charge. Mr. Lloyd-George, I am told, knowing the exact moment at which the mine was to be exploded, was awake, at home in England, and heard it, across the channel, and so did many folk who did not have his exceptional sources of information. I was one of them! And I wondered greatly until I was told what had been done. That was one of the most brilliantly and successfully executed attacks of the whole war, and vastly important in its results, although it was, compared to the great battles on the Somme and up north, near Arras, only a small and minor operation.

We settled down, very quickly indeed, into a regular routine. Captain Godfrey was, for all the world, like the manager of a traveling company in America. He mapped out our routes, and he took care of all the details. No troupe, covering a long route of one night stands in the Western or Southern United States, ever worked harder than did Hogge, Adam and I – to say nothing of Godfrey and our soldier chauffeurs. We did not lie abed late in the mornings, but were up soon after daylight. Breakfast out of the way, we would find the cars waiting and be off.

We had, always, a definite route mapped out for the day, but we never adhered to it exactly. I was still particularly pleased with the idea of giving a roadside concert whenever an audience appeared, and there was no lack of willing listeners. Soon after we had set out from Tramecourt, no matter in which direction we happened to be going, we were sure to run into some body of soldiers.

There was no longer any need of orders. As soon as the chauffeur of the leading car spied a blotch of khaki against the road, on went his brakes, and we would come sliding into the midst of the troops and stop. Johnson would be out before his car had fairly stopped, and at work upon the lashings of the little piano, with me to help him. And Hogge would already be clearing his throat to begin his speech.

The Reverend Harry Lauder, M.P., Tour, employed no press agent, and it could not boast of a bill poster. No hoardings were covered with great colored sheets advertising its coming. And yet the whole front seemed to know that we were about. The soldiers we met along the roads welcomed us gladly, but they were no longer, after the first day or two, surprised to see us. They acted, rather, as if they had been expecting us. Our advent was like that of a circus, coming to a country town for a long heralded and advertised engagement. Yet all the puffing that we got was by word of mouth.

There were some wonderful choruses along those war-worn roads we traveled. "Roamin' in the Gloamin'" was still my featured song, and all the soldiers seemed to know the tune and the words, and to take a particular delight in coming in with me as I swung into the chorus. We never passed a detachment of soldiers without stopping to give them a concert, no matter how it disarranged Captain Godfrey's plans.

But he was entirely willing. It was these men, on their way to the trenches, or on the way out of them, bound for rest billets, whom, of course, I was most anxious to reach, since I felt that they were the ones I was most likely to be able to help and cheer up.

The scheduled concerts were practically all at the various rest billets we visited. These were, in the main, at châteaux. Always, at such a place, I had a double audience. The soldiers would make a great ring, as close to me as they could get, and around them, again, in a sort of outer circle, were French villagers and peasants, vastly puzzled and mystified, but eager to be pleased, and very ready with their applause.

It must have been hard for them to make up their minds about me, if they gave me much thought. My kilt confused them; most of them thought I was a soldier from some regiment they had not yet seen, wearing a new and strange uniform. For my kilt, I need not say, was not military, nor was the rest of my garb warlike!

I gave, during that time, as many as seven concerts in a day. I have sung as often as thirty-five times in one day, and on such occasions I was thankful that I had a strong and durable voice, not easily worn out, as well as a stout physique. Hogge and Dr. Adam appeared as often as I did, but they didn't have to sing!

Nearly all the songs I gave them were ditties they had known for a long time. The one exception was the tune that had been so popular in "Three Cheers" – the one called "The Ladies Who Fought and Won." Few of the boys had been home since I had been singing that song, but it has a catching lilt, and they were soon able to join in the chorus and send it thundering along. They took to it, too – and well they might! It was of such as they that it was written.

We covered perhaps a hundred miles a day during this period. That does not sound like a great distance for high-powered motor cars, but we did a good deal of stopping, you see, here and there and everywhere. We were roaming around in the backwater of war, you might say. We were out of the main stream of carnage, but it was not out of our minds and our hearts. Evidences of it in plenty came to us each day. And each day we were a little nearer to the front line trenches than we had come the day before. We were working gradually toward that climax that I had been promised.

I was always eager to talk to officers and men, and I found many chances to do so. It seemed to me that I could never learn enough about the soldiers. I listened avidly to every story that was told to me, and was always asking for more. The younger officers, especially, it interested me to talk with. One day I was talking to such a lieutenant.

"How is the spirit of your men?" I asked him. I am going to tell you his answer, just as he made it.

"Their spirit?" he said, musingly. "Well, just before we came to this billet to rest we were in a tightish corner on the Somme. One of my youngest men was hit – a shell came near to taking his arm clean off, so that it was left just hanging to his shoulders. He was only about eighteen years old, poor chap. It was a bad wound, but, as sometimes happens, it didn't make him unconscious – then. And when he realized what had happened to him, and saw his arm hanging limp, so that he could know he was bound to lose it, he began to cry.

"'What's the trouble?' I asked him, hurrying over to him. I was sorry enough for him, but you've got to keep up the morale of your men. 'Soldiers don't cry when they're wounded, my lad.'

"'I'm not crying because I'm wounded, sir!' he fired back at me. And I won't say he was quite as respectful as a private is supposed to be when he's talking to an officer! 'Just take a look at that, sir!' And he pointed to his wound. And then he cried out:

"'And I haven't killed a German yet!' he said, bitterly. 'Isn't that hard lines, sir?'

"That is the spirit of my men!"

I made many good friends while I was roaming around the country just behind the front. I wonder how many of them I shall keep – how many of them death will spare to shake my hand again when peace is restored! There was a Gordon Highlander, a fine young officer, of whom I became particularly fond while I was at Tramecourt. I had a very long talk with him, and I thought of him often, afterward, because he made me think of John. He was just such a fine young type of Briton as my boy had been.

Months later, when I was back in Britain, and giving a performance at Manchester, there was a knock at the door of my dressing-room.

"Come in!" I called.

The door was pushed open and a man came in with great blue glasses covering his eyes. He had a stick, and he groped his way toward me. I did not know him at all at first – and then, suddenly, with a shock, I recognized him as my fine young Gordon Highlander of the rest billet near Tramecourt.

"My God – it's you, Mac!" I said, deeply shocked.

"Yes," he said, quietly. His voice had changed, greatly. "Yes, it's I, Harry."

He was almost totally blind, and he did not know whether his eyes would get better or worse.

"Do you remember all the lads you met at the billet where you came to sing for us the first time I met you, Harry?" he asked me. "Well, they're all gone – I'm the only one who's left – the only one!"

There was grief in his voice. But there was nothing like complaint, nor was there, nor self-pity, either, when he told me about his eyes and his doubts as to whether he would ever really see again. He passed his own troubles off lightly, as if they did not matter at all. He preferred to tell me about those of his friends whom I had met, and to give me the story of how this one and that one had gone. And he is like many another. I know a great many men who have been maimed in the war, but I have still to hear one of them complain. They were brave enough, God knows, in battle, but I think they are far braver when they come home, shattered and smashed, and do naught but smile at their troubles.

The only sort of complaining you hear from British soldiers is over minor discomforts in the field. Tommy and Jock will grouse when they are so disposed. They will growl about the food and about this trivial trouble and that. But it is never about a really serious matter that you hear them talking!

I have never yet met a man who had been permanently disabled who was not grieving because he could not go back. And it is strange but true that men on leave get homesick for the trenches sometimes. They miss the companionships they have had in the trenches. I think it must be because all the best men in the world are in France that they feel so. But it is true, I know, because I have not heard it once, but a dozen times.

Men will dream of home and Blighty for weeks and months. They will grouse because they cannot get leave – though, half the time, they have not even asked for it, because they feel that their place is where the fighting is! And then, when they do get that longed-for leave, they are half sorry to go – and they come back like boys coming home from school!

A great reward awaits the men who fight through this war and emerge alive and triumphant at its end. They will dictate the conduct of the world for many a year. The men who stayed at home when they should have gone may as well prepare to drop their voices to a very low whisper in the affairs of mankind. For the men who will be heard, who will make themselves heard, are out there in France.

CHAPTER XX

It was seven o'clock in the morning of a Godly and a beautiful day when we set out from Tramecourt for Arras. Arras, that town so famous now in British history and in the annals of this war, had been one of our principal objectives from the outset, but we had not known when we were to see it. Arras had been the pivot of the great northern drive in the spring – the drive that Hindenburg had fondly supposed he had spoiled by his "strategic" retreat in the region of the Somme, begun just before the British and the French were ready to attack.

What a bonnie morning that was, to be sure! The sun was out, after some rainy days, and glad we all were to see it. The land was sprayed with silver light; the air was as sweet and as soft and as warm as a baby's breath. And the cars seemed to leap forward, as if they, too, loved the day and the air. They ate up the road. They seemed to take hold of its long, smooth surface – they are grand roads, over yon, in France – and reel it up in underneath their wheels as if it were a tape.

This time we did little stopping, no matter how good the reason looked. We went hurtling through villages and towns we had not seen before. Our horn and our siren shrieked a warning as we shot through. And it seemed wrong. They looked so peaceful and so quiet, did those French towns, on that summer's morning! Peaceful, aye, and languorous, after all the bustle and haste we had been seeing. The houses were set in pretty encasements of bright foliage and they looked as though they had been painted against the background of the landscape with water colors.

It was hard to believe that war had passed that way. It had; there were traces everywhere of its grim visitation. But here its heavy hand had been laid lightly upon town and village. It was as if a wave of poison gas of the sort the Germans brought into war had been turned aside by a friendly breeze, arising in the very nick of time. Little harm had been done along the road we traveled. But the thunder of the guns was always in our ears; we could hear the steady, throbbing rhythm of the cannon, muttering away to the north and east.

It was very warm, and so, after a time, as we passed through a village, someone – Hogge, I think – suggested that a bottle of ginger beer all around would not be amiss. The idea seemed to be regarded as an excellent one, so Godfrey spoke to the chauffeur beside him, and we stopped. We had not known, at first, that there were troops in town. But there were – Highlanders. And they came swarming out. I was recognized at once.

"Well, here's old Harry Lauder!" cried one braw laddie.

"Come on, Harry – gie us a song!" they shouted. "Let's have 'Roamin' in the Gloamin', Harry! Gie us the Bonnie Lassie! We ha' na' heard 'The Laddies Who Fought and Won,' Harry. They tell us that's a braw song!"

We were not really supposed to give any roadside concerts that day, but how was I to resist them? So we pulled up into a tiny side street, just off the market square, and I sang several songs for them. We saved time by not unlimbering the wee piano, and I sang, without accompaniment, standing up in the car. But they seemed to be as well pleased as though I had had the orchestra of a big theater to support me, and all the accompaniments and trappings of the stage. They were very loath to let me go, and I don't know how much time we really saved by not giving our full and regular programme. For, before I had done, they had me telling stories, too. Captain Godfrey was smiling, but he was glancing at his watch too, and he nudged me, at last, and made me realize that it was time for us to go on, no matter how interesting it might be to stay.

"I'll be good," I promised, with a grin, as we drove on. "We shall go straight on to Arras now!"

But we did not. We met a bunch of engineers on the road, after a space, and they looked so wistful when we told them we maun be getting right along, without stopping to sing for them, that I had not the heart to disappoint them. So we got out the wee piano and I sang them a few songs. It seemed to mean so much to those boys along the roads! I think they enjoyed the concerts even more than did the great gatherings that were assembled for me at the rest camps. A concert was more of a surprise for them, more of a treat. The other laddies liked them, too – aye, they liked them fine. But they would have been prepared, sometimes; they would have been looking forward to the fun. And the laddies along the roads took them as a man takes a grand bit of scenery, coming before his eyes, suddenly, as he turns a bend in a road he does not ken.

As for myself, I felt that I was becoming quite a proficient open-air performer by now. My voice was standing the strain of singing under such novel and difficult conditions much better than I had thought it could. And I saw that I must be at heart and by nature a minstrel! I know I got more pleasure from those concerts I gave as a minstrel wandering in France than did the soldiers or any of those who heard me!

I have been before the public for many years. Applause has always been sweet to me. It is to any artist, and when one tells you it is not you may set it down in your hearts that he or she is telling less than the truth. It is the breath of life to us to know that folks are pleased by what we do for them. Why else would we go on about our tasks? I have had much applause. I have had many honors. I have told you about that great and overwhelming reception that greeted me when I sailed into Sydney Harbor. In Britain, in America, I have had greetings that have brought tears into my eye and such a lump into my throat that until it had gone down I could not sing or say a word of thanks.

But never has applause sounded so sweet to me as it did along those dusty roads in France, with the poppies gleaming red and the cornflowers blue through the yellow fields of grain beside the roads! They cheered me, do you ken – those tired and dusty heroes of Britain along the French roads! They cheered as they squatted down in a circle about us, me in my kilt, and Johnson tinkling away as if his very life depended upon it, at his wee piano! Ah, those wonderful, wonderful soldiers! The tears come into my eyes, and my heart is sore and heavy within me when I think that mine was the last voice many of them ever heard lifted in song! They were on their way to the trenches, so many of those laddies who stopped for a song along the road. And when men are going into the trenches they know, and all who see them passing know, that some there are who will never come out.

Despite all the interruptions, though, it was not much after noon when we reached Blangy. Here, in that suburb of Arras, were the headquarters of the Ninth Division, and as I stepped out of the car I thrilled to the knowledge that I was treading ground forever to be famous as the starting-point of the Highland Brigade in the attack of April 9, 1917.

And now I saw Arras, and, for the first time, a town that had been systematically and ruthlessly shelled. There are no words in any tongue I know to give you a fitting picture of the devastation of Arras. "Awful" is a puny word, a thin one, a feeble one. I pick impotently at the cover-lid of my imagination when I try to frame language to make you understand what it was I saw when I came to Arras on that bright June day.

I think the old city of Arras should never be rebuilt. I doubt if it can be rebuilt, indeed. But I think that, whether or no, a golden fence should be built around it, and it should forever and for all time be preserved as a monument to the wanton wickedness of the Hun. It should serve and stand, in its stark desolation, as a tribute, dedicated to the Kultur of Germany. No painter could depict the frightfulness of that city of the dead. No camera could make you see as it is. Only your eyes can do that for you. And even then you cannot realize it all at once. Your eyes are more merciful than the truth and the Hun.

The Germans shelled Arras long after there was any military reason for doing so. The sheer, wanton love of destruction must have moved them. They had destroyed its military usefulness, but still they poured shot and shell into the town. I went through its streets – the Germans had been pushed back so far by then that the city was no longer under steady fire. But they had done their work!

Nobody was living in Arras. No one could have lived there. The houses had been smashed to pieces. The pavements were dust and rubble. But there was life in the city. Through the ruins our men moved as ceaselessly and as restlessly as the tenants of an ant hill suddenly upturned by a plowshare. Soldiers were everywhere, and guns – guns, guns! For Arras had a new importance now. It was a center for many roads. Some of the most important supply roads of this sector of the front converged in Arras.

Trains of ammunition trucks, supply carts and wagons of all sorts, great trucks laden with jam and meat and flour, all were passing every moment. There was an incessant din of horses' feet and the steady crunch – crunch of heavy boots as the soldiers marched through the rubble and the brickdust. And I knew that all this had gone on while the town was still under fire. Indeed, even now, an occasional shell from some huge gun came crashing into the town, and there would be a new cloud of dust arising to mark its landing, a new collapse of some weakened wall. Warning signs were everywhere about, bidding all who saw them to beware of the imminent collapse of some heap of masonry.

I saw what the Germans had left of the stately old Cathedral, and of the famous Cloth Hall – one of the very finest examples of the guild halls of medieval times. Goths – Vandals – no, it is unfair to seek such names for the Germans. They have established themselves as the masters of all time in brutality and in destruction. There is no need to call them anything but Germans. The Cloth Hall was almost human in its pitiful appeal to the senses and the imagination. The German fire had picked it to pieces, so that it stood in a stark outline, like some carcass picked bare by a vulture.

Our soldiers who were quartered nearby lived outside the town in huts. They were the men of the Highland Brigade, and the ones I had hoped and wished, above all others, to meet when I came to France. They received our party with the greatest enthusiasm, and they were especially flattering when they greeted me. One of the Highland officers took me in hand immediately, to show me the battlefield.

The ground over which we moved had literally been churned by shell-fire. It was neither dirt nor mud that we walked upon; it was a sort of powder. The very soil had been decomposed into a fine dust by the terrific pounding it had received. The dust rose and got into our eyes and mouths and nostrils. There was a lot of sneezing among the members of the Reverend Harry Lauder, M.P., Tour that day at Arras! And the wire! It was strewn in every direction, with seeming aimlessness. Heavily barbed it was, and bad stuff to get caught in. One of the great reasons for the preliminary bombardment that usually precedes an attack is to cut this wire. If charging men are caught in a bad tangle of wire they can be wiped out by machine gun-fire before they can get clear.

I asked a Highlander, one day, how long he thought the war would last.

"Forty years," he said, never batting an eyelid. "We'll be fighting another year, and then it'll tak us thirty-nine years more to wind up all the wire!"

Off to my right there was a network of steel strands, and as I gazed at it I saw a small dark object hanging from it and fluttering in the breeze. I was curious enough to go over, and I picked my way carefully through the maze-like network of wire to see what it might be. When I came close I saw it was a bit of cloth, and immediately I recognized the tartan of the Black Watch – the famous Forty-second. Mud and blood held that bit of cloth fastened to the wire, as if by a cement. Plainly, it had been torn from a kilt.

I stood for a moment, looking down at that bit of tartan, flapping in the soft summer breeze. And as I stood I could look out and over the landscape, dotted with a very forest of little wooden crosses, that marked the last resting-place of the men who had charged across this maze of wire and died within it. They rose, did those rough crosses, like sheathed swords out of the wild, luxurious jungle of grass that had grown up in that blood-drenched soil. I wondered if the owner of the bit of tartan were still safe or if he lay under one of the crosses that I saw.

There was room for sad speculation here! Who had he been? Had he swept on, leaving that bit of his kilt as evidence of his passing? Had he been one of those who had come through the attack, gloriously, to victory, so that he could look back upon that day so long as he lived? Or was he dead – perhaps within a hundred yards of where I stood and gazed down at that relic of him? Had he folks at hame in Scotland who had gone through days of anguish on his account – such days of anguish as I had known?

I asked a soldier for some wire clippers, and I cut the wire on either side of that bit of tartan, and took it, just as it was. And as I put the wee bit of a brave man's kilt away I kissed the blood-stained tartan, for Auld Lang Syne, and thought of what a tale it could tell if it could only speak!

> "Ha' ye seen a' the men frae the braes and the glen,
>   Ha' ye seen them a' marchin' awa'?
> Ha' ye seen a' the men frae the wee but-an'-ben,
>   And the gallants frae mansion and ha'?"

I have said before that I do not want to tell you of the tales of atrocities that I heard in France. I heard plenty – aye and terrible they were! But I dinna wish to harrow the feelings of those who read more than I need, and I will leave that task to those who saw for themselves with their eyes, when I had but my ears to serve me. Yet there was one blood-chilling story that my boy John told to me, and that the finding of that bit of Black Watch tartan brings to my mind. He told it to me as we sat before the fire in my wee hoose at Dunoon, just a few nights before he went back to the front for the last time. We were talking of the war – what else was there to talk aboot?

It was seldom that John touched on the harsher things he knew about the war. He preferred, as a rule, to tell me stories of the courage and the devotion of his men, and of the light way that they turned things when there was so much chance for grief and care.

"One night, Dad," he said, "we had a battalion of the Black Watch on our right, and they made a pretty big raid on the German trenches. It developed into a sizable action for any other war, but one trifling enough and unimportant in this one. The Germans had been readier than the Black Watch had supposed, and had reinforcements ready, and sixty of the Highlanders were captured. The Germans took them back into their trenches, and stripped them to the skin. Not a stitch or a rag of clothing did they leave them, and, though it was April, it was a bitter night, with a wind to cut even a man warmly clad to the bone.

"All night they kept them there, standing at attention, stark naked, so that they were half-frozen when the gray, cold light of the dawn began to show behind them in the east. And then the Germans laughed, and told their prisoners to go.

'Go on – go back to your own trenches, as you are!' they said.

"The laddies of the Black Watch could scarcely believe their ears. There was about seventy-five yards between the two trench lines at that point, and the No Man's Land was rough going – all shell-pitted as it was. By that time, too, of course, German repair parties had mended all the wire before their trenches. So they faced a rough journey, all naked as they were. But they started.

"They got through the wire, with the Germans laughing fit to kill themselves at the sight of the streaks of blood showing on their white skins as the wire got in its work. They laughed at them, Dad! And then, when they were halfway across the No Man's Land they understood, at last, why the Germans had let them go. For fire was opened on them with machine guns. Everyone was mowed down – everyone of those poor, naked, bleeding lads was killed – murdered by that treacherous fire from behind!

"We heard all the details of that dirty bit of treachery later. We captured some German prisoners from that very trench. Fritz is a decent enough sort, sometimes, and there were men there whose stomachs were turned by that sight, so that they were glad to creep over, later, and surrender. They told us, with tears in their eyes. But we had known, before that. We had needed no witnesses except the bodies of the boys. It had been too dark for the men in our trenches to see what was going on – and a burst of machine gun-fire, along the trenches, is nothing to get curious or excited about. But those naked bodies, lying there in the No Man's Land, had told us a good deal.

"Dad – that was an awful sight! I was in command of one of the burying parties we had to send out."

That was the tale I thought of when I found that bit of the Black Watch tartan. And I remembered, too, that it was with the Black Watch that John Poe, the famous

American football player from Princeton, met his death in a charge. He had been offered a commission, but he preferred to stay with the boys in the ranks.

CHAPTER XXI

We left our motor cars behind us in Arras, for to-day we were to go to a front-line trench, and the climax of my whole trip, so far as I could foresee, was at hand. Johnson and the wee piano had to stay behind, too – we could not expect to carry even so tiny an instrument as that into a front-line trench! Once more we had to don steel helmets, but there was a great difference between these and the ones we had had at Vimy Ridge. Mine fitted badly, and kept sliding down over my ears, or else slipping way down to the back of my head. It must have given me a grotesque look, and it was most uncomfortable. So I decided I would take it off and carry it for a while.

"You'd better keep it on, Harry," Captain Godfrey advised me. "This district is none too safe, even right here, and it gets worse as we go along. A whistling Percy may come along looking for you any minute."

That is the name of a shell that is good enough to advertise its coming by a whistling, shrieking sound. I could hear Percies whistling all around, and see them spattering up the ground as they struck, not so far away, but they did not seem to be coming in our direction. So I decided I would take a chance.

"Well," I said, as I took the steel hat off, "I'll just keep this bonnet handy and slip it on if I see Percy coming."

But later I was mighty glad of even an ill-fitting steel helmet!

Several staff officers from the Highland Brigade had joined the Reverend Harry Lauder, M.P., Tour by now. Affable, pleasant gentlemen they were, and very eager to show us all there was to be seen. And they had more sights to show their visitors than most hosts have!

We were on ground now that had been held by the Germans before the British had surged forward all along this line in the April battle. Their old trenches, abandoned now, ran like deep fissures through the soil. They had been pretty well blasted to pieces by the British bombardment, but a good many of their deep, concrete dugouts had survived. These were not being used by the British here, but were saved in good repair as show places, and the officers who were our guides took us down into some of them.

Rarely comfortable they must have been, too! They had been the homes of German officers, and the Hun officers did themselves very well indeed when they had the chance. They had electric light in their cave houses. To be sure they had used German wall paper, and atrociously ugly stuff it was, too. But it pleased their taste, no doubt. Mightily amazed some of Fritz's officers must have been, back in April, as they sat and took their ease in these luxurious quarters, to have Jock come tumbling in upon them, a grenade in each hand!

Our men might have used these dugouts, and been snug enough in them, but they preferred air and ventilation, and lived in little huts above the ground. I left our party and went around among them and, to my great satisfaction, found, as I had been pretty sure I would, a number of old acquaintances and old admirers who came crowding around me to shake hands. I made a great collection of souvenirs here, for they insisted on pressing trophies upon me.

"Tak them, Harry," said one after another. "We can get plenty more where they came from!"

One laddie gave me a helmet with a bullet hole through the skip, and another presented me with one of the most interesting souvenirs of all I carried home from France. That was a German sniper's outfit. It consisted of a suit of overalls, waterproofed. If a man had it on he would be completely covered, from head to foot, with just a pair of slits for his eyes to peep out of, and another for his mouth, so that he could breathe. It was cleverly painted the color of a tree – part of it like the bark, part green, like leaves sprouting from it.

"Eh, Jock," I asked the laddie who gave it to me. "A thing like yon's hard to be getting, I'm thinking?"

"Oh, not so very hard," he answered, carelessly. "You've got to be a good shot." And he wore medals that showed he was! "All you've got to do, Harry, is to kill the chap inside it before he kills you! The fellow who used to own that outfit you've got hid himself in the fork of a tree, and, as you may guess, he looked like a branch of the tree itself. He was pretty hard to spot. But I got suspicious of him, from the way bullets were coming over steadily, and I decided that that tree hid a sniper.

"After that it was just a question of being patient. It was no so long before I was sure, and then I waited – until I saw that branch move as no branch of a tree ever did move. I fired then – and got him! He was away outside of his lines, and that nicht I slipped out and brought back this outfit. I wanted to see how it was made."

An old, grizzled sergeant of the Black Watch gave me a German revolver.

"How came you to get this?" I asked him.

"It was an acceedent, Harry," he said. "We were raiding a trench, do you ken, and I was in a sap when a German officer came along, and we bumped into one another. He looked at me, and I at him. I think he was goin' to say something, but I dinna ken what it was he had on his mind. That *was* his revolver you've got in your hand now."

And then he thrust his hand into his pocket.

"Here's the watch he used to carry, too," he said. It was a thick, fat-bellied affair, of solid gold. "It's a bit too big, but it's a rare good timekeeper."

Soon after that an officer gave me another trophy that is, perhaps, even more interesting than the sniper's suit. It is rarer, at least. It is a small, sweet-toned bell that used to hang in a wee church in the small village of Athies, on the Scarpe, about a mile and a half from Arras. The Germans wiped out church and village, but in some odd way they found the bell and saved it. They hung it in their trenches, and it was used to sound a gas alarm. On both sides a signal is given when the sentry sees that there is to be a gas attack, in order that the men may have time to don the clumsy gas masks that are the only protection against the deadly fumes. The wee bell is eight inches high, maybe, and I have never heard a lovelier tone.

"That bell has rung men to worship, and it has rung them to death," said the officer who gave it to me.

Presently I was called back to my party, after I had spent some time with the lads in their huts. A general had joined the party now, and he told me, with a smile, that I was to go up to the trenches, if I cared to do so. I will not say I was not a bit nervous, but I was glad to go, for a' that! It was the thing that had brought me to France, after a'.

So we started, and by now I was glad to wear my steel hat, fit or no fit. I was to give an entertainment in the trenches, and so we set out. Pretty soon I was climbing a steep railroad embankment, and when we slid down on the other side we found the trenches – wide, deep gaps in the earth, and all alive with men. We got into the trenches themselves by means of ladders, and the soldiers came swarming about me with yells of "Hello, Harry! Welcome, Harry!"

They were told that I had come to sing for them, and so, with no further preliminaries, I began my concert. I started with my favorite opening song, as usual – "Roamin' in the Gloamin'," and then went on with the other old favorites. I told a lot of stories, too, and then I came to "The Laddies Who Fought and Won." None of the men had heard it, but there were officers there who had seen "Three Cheers" during the winter when they had had a short leave to run over to London.

I got through the first verse all right, and was just swinging into the first chorus when, without the least warning, hell popped open in that trench. A missile came in that some officer at once hailed as a whizz bang. It is called that, for that is just exactly the sound it makes. It is like a giant firecracker, and it would be amusing if one did not know it was deadly. These missiles are not fired by the big guns behind the lines, but by the small trench cannon – worked, as a rule, by compressed air. The range is very short, but they are capable of great execution at that range.

Was I frightened? I must have been! I know I felt a good deal as I have done when I have been seasick. And I began to think at once of all sorts of places where I would rather have been than in that trench! I was standing on a slight elevation at the back, or parados, of the trench, so that I was raised a bit above my audience, and I had a fine view of that deadly thing, wandering about, spitting fire and metal parts. It traveled so that the men could dodge it, but it was throwing oft slugs that you could neither see nor dodge, and it was a poor place to be!

And the one whizz bang was not enough to suit Fritz. It was followed immediately by a lot more, that came popping in and making themselves as unpleasant as you could imagine. I watched the men about me, and they seemed to be unconcerned, and to be thinking much more of me and my singing than of the whizz bangs. So, no matter how I felt, there was nothing for me to do but to keep on with my song. I decided that I must really be safe enough, no matter how I felt. But I had certain misgivings on the subject. Still, I managed to go on with my song, and I think I was calm enough to look at – though, if I was, my appearance wholly belied my true inward feelings.

I struggled through to the end of the chorus – and I think I sang pretty badly, although I don't know. But I was pretty sure the end of the world had come for me, and that these laddies were taking things as calmly as they were simply because they were used to it, and it was all in the day's work for them. The Germans were fairly sluicing that trench by now. The whizz bangs were popping over us like giant fire-crackers, going off one and two and three at a time. And the trench was full of flying slugs and chunks of dirt, striking against our faces and hurtling all about us.

There I was. I had a good "house." I wanted to please my audience. Was it no a trying situation? I thought Fritz might have had manners enough to wait until I had finished my concert, at least! But the Hun has no manners, as all the world knows.

Along that embankment we had climbed to reach the trenches, and not very far from the bit of trench in which I was singing, there was a railroad bridge of some strategic importance. And now a shell hit that bridge – not a whizz bang, but a real, big shell. It exploded with a hideous screech, as if the bridge were some human thing being struck, and screaming out its agony. The soldiers looked at me, and I saw some of them winking. They seemed to be mighty interested in the way I was taking all this. I looked back at them, and then at a Highland colonel who was listening to my singing as quietly and as carefully as if he had been at a stall in Covent Garden during the opera season. He caught my glance.

"I think they're coming it a bit thick, Lauder, old chap," he remarked, quietly.

"I quite agree with you, colonel," I said. I tried to ape his voice and manner, but I wasn't so quiet as he.

Now there came a ripping, tearing sound in the air, and a veritable cloudburst of the damnable whizz bangs broke over us. That settled matters. There were no orders, but everyone turned, just as if it were a meeting, and a motion to adjourn had been put and carried unanimously. We all ran for the safety holes or dug-outs in the side of the embankment. And I can tell ye that the Reverend Harry Lauder, M.P., Tour were no the last ones to reach those shelters! No, we were by no means the last!

I ha' no doot that I might have improved upon the shelter that I found, had I had time to pick and choose. But any shelter was good just then, and I was glad of mine, and of a chance to catch my breath. Afterward, I saw a picture by Captain Bairnsfather that made me laugh a good deal, because it represented so exactly the way I felt. He had made a drawing of two Tommies in a wee bit of a hole in a field that was being swept by shells and missiles of every sort. One was grousing to his mate, and the other said to him:

"If you know a better 'ole go 'ide in it!"

I said we all turned and ran for cover. But there was one braw laddie who did nothing of the sort. He would not run – such tricks were not for him!

He was a big Hie'land laddie, and he wore naught but his kilt and his semmet – his undershirt. He had on his steel helmet, and it shaded a face that had not been shaved or washed for days. His great, brawny arms were folded across his chest, and he was smoking his pipe. And he stood there as quiet and unconcerned as if he had been a village smith gazing down a quiet country road. I watched him, and he saw me, and grinned at me. And now and then he glanced at me, quizzically.

"It's all right, Harry," he said, several times. "Dinna fash yoursel', man. I'll tell ye in time for ye to duck if I see one coming your way!"

We crouched in our holes until there came a brief lull in the bombardment. Probably the Germans thought they had killed us all and cleared the trench, or maybe it had been only that they hadn't liked my singing, and had been satisfied when they had stopped it. So we came out, but the firing was not over at all, as we found out at once. So we went down a bit deeper, into concrete dugouts.

This trench had been a part of the intricate German defensive system far back of their old front line, and they had had the pains of building and hollowing out the fine dugout into which I now went for shelter. Here they had lived, deep under the earth, like animals – and with animals, too. For when I reached the bottom a dog came to meet me, sticking out his red tongue to lick my hand, and wagging his tail as friendly as you please.

He was a German dog – one of the prisoners of war taken in the great attack. His old masters hadn't bothered to call him and take him with them when the

Highlanders came along, and so he had stayed behind as part of the spoils of the attack.

That wasn't much of a dog, as dogs go. He was a mongrel-looking creature, but he couldn't have been friendlier. The Highlanders had adopted him and called him Fritz, and they were very fond of him, and he of them. He had no thought of war. He behaved just as dogs do at hame.

But above us the horrid din was still going on, and bits of shells were flying everywhere – any one of them enough to kill you, if it struck you in the right spot. I was glad, I can tell ye, that I was so snug and safe beneath the ground, and I had no mind at all to go out until the bombardment was well over. I knew now what it was really to be under fire. The casual sort of shelling I had had to fear at Vimy Ridge was nothing to this. This was the real thing.

And then I thought that what I was experiencing for a few minutes was the daily portion of these laddies who were all aboot me – not for a few minutes, but for days and weeks and months at a time. And it came home to me again, and stronger than ever, what they were doing for us folks at hame, and how we ought to be feeling for them.

The heavy firing went on for three-quarters of an hour, at least. We could hear the chugging of the big guns, and the sorrowful swishing of the shells, as if they were mournful because they were not wreaking more destruction than they were. It all moved me greatly, but I could see that the soldiers thought nothing of it, and were quite unperturbed by the fearful demonstration that was going on above. They smoked and chatted, and my own nerves grew calmer.

Finally there seemed to come a real lull in the row above, and I turned to the general.

"Isn't it near time for me to be finishing my concert, sir?" I asked him.

"Very good," he said, jumping up. "Just as you say, Lauder."

So back we went to where I had begun to sing. My audience reassembled, and I struck up "The Laddies Who Fought and Won" again. It seemed, somehow, the most appropriate song I could have picked to sing in that spot! I finished, this time, but there was some discord in the closing bars, for the Germans were still at their shelling, sporadically.

So I finished, and I said good-by to the men who were to stay in the trench, guarding that bit of Britain's far flung battleline. And then the Reverend Harry Lauder, M.P., Tour was ready to go back – not to safety, at once, but to a region far less infested by the Hun than this one where we had been such warmly received visitors!

CHAPTER XXII

I was sorry to be leaving the Highland laddies in that trench. Aye! But for the trench itself I had nae regrets – nae, none whatever! I know no spot on the surface of this earth, of all that I have visited, and I have been in many climes, that struck me as less salubrious than yon bit o' trench. There were too many other visitors there that day, along with the Reverend Harry Lauder, M.P., Tour. They were braw laddies, yon, but no what you might call over-particular about the company they kept! I'd thank them, if they'd be havin' me to veesit them again, to let me come by my ain!

Getting away was not the safest business in the world, either, although it was better than staying in yon trench. We had to make our way back to the railway embankment, and along it for a space, and the embankment was being heavily shelled. It was really a trench line itself, full of dugouts, and as we made our way along heads popped in all directions, topped by steel helmets. I was eager to be on the other side of you embankment, although I knew well enough that there was no sanctuary on either side of it, nor for a long space behind it.

That was what they called the Frenchy railway cutting, and it overlooked the ruined village of Athies. And not until after I had crossed it was I breathing properly. I began, then, to feel more like myself, and my heart and all my functions began to be more normal.

All this region we had to cross now was still under fire, but the fire was nothing to what it had been. The evidences of the terrific bombardments there had been were plainly to be seen. Every scrap of exposed ground had been nicked by shells; the holes were as close together as those in a honeycomb. I could not see how any living thing had come through that hell of fire, but many men had. Now the embankment fairly buzzed with activity. The dugouts were everywhere, and the way the helmeted heads popped out as we passed, inquiringly, made me think of the prairie dog towns I had seen in Canada and the western United States.

The river Scarpe flowed close by. It was a narrow, sluggish stream, and it did not look to me worthy of its famous name. But often, that spring, its slow-moving waters had been flecked by a bloody froth, and the bodies of brave men had been hidden by them, and washed clean of the trench mud. Now, uninviting as its aspect was, and sinister as were the memories it must have evoked in other hearts beside my own, it was water. And on so hot a day water was a precious thing to men who had been working as the laddies hereabout had worked and labored.

So either bank was dotted with naked bodies, and the stream itself showed head after head, and flashing white arms as men went swimming. Some were scrubbing themselves, taking a Briton's keen delight in a bath, no matter what the circumstances in which he gets it; others were washing their clothes, slapping and pounding the soaked garments in a way to have wrung the hearts of their wives, had they seen them at it. The British soldier, in the field, does many things for himself that folks at hame never think of! But many of the men were just lying on the bank, sprawled out and sunning themselves like alligators, basking in the warm sunshine and soaking up rest and good cheer.

It looked like a good place for a concert, and so I quickly gathered an audience of about a thousand men from the dugouts in the embankment and obeyed their injunctions to "Go it, Harry! Gie us a song, do now!"

As I finished my first song my audience applauded me and cheered me most heartily, and the laddies along the banks of the Scarpe heard them, and came running up to see what was afoot. There were no ladies thereabout, and they did not stand on a small matter like getting dressed! Not they! They came running just as they were, and Adam, garbed in his fig leaf, was fully clad compared to most of them. It was the barest gallery I ever saw, and the noisiest, too, and the most truly appreciative.

High up above us airplanes were circling, so high that we could not tell from which side they came, except when we saw some of them being shelled, and so knew that they belonged to Fritz. They looked like black pinheads against the blue cushion of the sky, and no doubt that they were vastly puzzled as to the reason of this gathering of naked men. What new tricks were the damned English up to now? So I have no doubt, they were wondering! It was the business of their observers, of course, to spot just such gatherings as ours, although I did not think of that just then – except to think that they might drop a bomb or two, maybe.

But scouting airplanes, such as those were, do not go in for bomb dropping. There are three sorts of airplanes. First come the scouting planes – fairly fast, good climbers, able to stay in the air a long time. Their business is just to spy out the lay of the land over the enemy's trenches – not to fight or drop bombs. Then come the swift, powerful bombing planes, which make raids, flying long distances to do so. The Huns use such planes to bomb unprotected towns and kill women and babies; ours go in for bombing ammunition dumps and trains and railway stations and other places of military importance, although, by now, they may be indulging in reprisals for some of Fritz's murderous raids, as so many folk at hame in Britain have prayed they would.

Both scouting and bombing planes are protected by the fastest flyers of all – the battle planes, as they are called. These fight other planes in the air, and it is the men who steer them and fight their guns who perform the heroic exploits that you may read of every day. But much of the great work in the air is done by the scouting planes, which take desperate chances, and find it hard to fight back when they are attacked. And it was scouts who were above us now – and, doubtless, sending word back by wireless of a new and mysterious concentration of

British forces along the Scarpe, which it might be a good thing for the Hun artillery to strafe a bit!

So, before very long, a rude interruption came to my songs, in the way of shells dropped unpleasantly close. The men so far above us had given their guns the range, and so, although the gunners could not see us, they could make their presence felt.

I have never been booed or hissed by an audience, since I have been on the stage. I understand that it is a terrible and a disconcerting experience, and one calculated to play havoc with the stoutest of nerves. It is an experience I am by no means anxious to have, I can tell you! But I doubt if it could seem worse to me than the interruption of a shell. The Germans, that day, showed no ear for music, and no appreciation of art – my art, at least!

And so it seemed well to me to cut my programme, to a certain extent, at least, and bid farewell to my audience, dressed and undressed. It was a performance at which it did not seem to me a good idea to take any curtain calls. I did not miss them, nor feel slighted because they were absent. I was too glad to get away with a whole skin!

The shelling became very furious now. Plainly the Germans meant to take no chances. They couldn't guess what the gathering their airplanes had observed might portend, but, if they could, they meant to defeat its object, whatever that might be. Well, they did not succeed, but they probably had the satisfaction of thinking that they had, and I, for one, do not begrudge them that. They forced the Reverend Harry Lauder, M.P., Tour to make a pretty wide detour, away from the river, to get back to the main road. But they fired a power of shells to do so!

When we finally reached the road I heard a mad sputtering behind. I looked around in alarm, because it sounded, for all the world, like one of those infernal whizz bangs, chasing me. But it was not. The noise came from a motor cycle, and its rider dashed up to me and dropped one foot to the ground.

"Here's a letter for you, Harry," he said.

It was a package that he handed me. I was surprised – I was not expecting to have a post delivered to me on the battlefield of Arras! It turned out that the package contained a couple of ugly-looking bits of shell, and a letter from my friends the Highlanders on the other side of the railway embankment. They wrote to thank me for singing for them, and said they hoped I was none the worse for the bombardment I had undergone.

"These bits of metal are from the shell that was closest to you when it burst," their spokesman wrote. "They nearly got you, and we thought you'd like to have them to keep for souvenirs."

It seemed to me that that was a singularly calm and phlegmatic letter! My nerves were a good deal overwrought, as I can see now.

Now we made our way slowly back to division headquarters, and there I found that preparations had been made for very much the most ambitious and pretentious concert that I had yet had a chance to give in France. There was a very large audience, and a stage or platform had been set up, with plenty of room on it for Johnson and his piano. It had been built in a great field, and all around me, when I mounted it, I could see kilted soldiers – almost as far as my eye could reach. There were many thousands of them there – indeed, all of the Highland Brigade that was not actually on duty at the moment was present, and a good many other men beside, for good measure.

Here was a sight to make a Scots heart leap with pride! Here, before me, was the flower of Scottish manhood. These regiments had been through a series of battles, not so long since, that had sadly thinned their ranks. Many a Scottish grave had been filled that spring; many a Scottish heart at hame had been broken by sad news from this spot. But there they were now, before me – their ranks filled up again, splendid as they stretched out, eager to welcome me and cheer me. There were tears in my eyes as I looked around at them.

Massed before me were all the best men Scotland had had to offer! All these men had breathed deep of the hellish air of war. All had marched shoulder to shoulder and skirt to skirt with death. All were of my country and my people. My heart was big within me with pride of them, and that I was of their race, as I stood up to sing for them.

Johnson was waiting for me to be ready. Little "Tinkle Tom," as we called the wee piano, was not very large, but there were times when he had to be left behind. I think he was glad to have us back again, and to be doing his part, instead of leaving me to sing alone, without his stout help.

Many distinguished officers were in that great assemblage. They all turned out to hear me, as well as the men, and among them I saw many familiar faces and old friends from hame. But there were many faces, too, alas, that I did not see. And when I inquired for them later I learned that many of them I had seen for the last time. Oh, the sad news I learned, day after day, oot there in France! Friend after friend of whom I made inquiry was known, to be sure. They could tell me where, and when, and how, they had been killed.

Up above us, as I began to sing, our airplanes were circling. No Boche planes were in sight now, I had been told, but there were many of ours. And sometimes one came swooping down, its occupants curious, no doubt, as to what might be going on, and the hum of its huge propeller would make me falter a bit in my song. And once or twice one flew so low and so close that I was almost afraid it would strike me, and I would dodge in what I think was mock alarm, much to the amusement of the soldiers.

I had given them two songs when a big man arose, far back in the crowd. He was a long way from me, but his great voice carried to me easily, so that I could hear every word he said.

"Harry," he shouted, "sing us 'The Wee Hoose Amang the Heather' and we'll a' join in the chorus!"

For a moment I could only stare out at them. Between that sea of faces, upraised to mine, and my eyes, there came another face – the smiling, bonnie face of my boy John, that I should never see again with mortal eyes. That had been one of his favorite songs for many years. I hesitated. It was as if a gentle hand had plucked at my very heart strings, and played upon them. Memory – memories of my boy, swept over me in a flood. I felt a choking in my throat, and the tears welled into my eyes.

But then I began to sing, making a signal to Johnson to let me sing alone. And when I came to the chorus, true to the big Highlander's promise, they all did join in the chorus! And what a chorus that was! Thousands of men were singing.

> "There's a wee hoose amang the heather,
> There's a wee hoose o'er the sea.
> There's a lassie in that wee hoose
> Waiting patiently for me.
> She's the picture of perfection –
> I would na tell a lee
> If ye saw her ye would love her
> Just the same as me!"

My voice was very shaky when I came to the end of that chorus, but the great wave of sound from the kilted laddies rolled out, true and full, unshaken, unbroken. They carried the air as steadily as a ship is carried upon a rolling sea.

I could sing no more for them, and then, as I made my way, unsteadily enough, from the platform, music struck up that was the sweetest I could have heard. Some pipers had come together, from twa or three regiments, unknown to me, and now, very softly, their pipes began to skirl. They played the tune that I love best, "The Drunken Piper." I could scarcely see to pick my way, for the tears that blinded me, but in my ears, as I passed away from them, there came, gently wailing on the pipes, the plaintive plea – "Will ye no come back again?"

CHAPTER XXIII

Now it was time to take to the motor cars again, and I was glad of the thought that we would have a bracing ride. I needed something of the sort, I thought. My emotions had been deeply stirred, in many ways, that day. I felt tired and quite exhausted. This was by all odds the most strenuous day the Reverend Harry Lauder, M.P., Tour had put in yet in France. So I welcomed the idea of sitting back comfortably in the car and feeling the cool wind against my cheeks.

First, however, the entertainers were to be entertained. They took us, the officers of the divisional staff, to a hut, where we were offered our choice of tea or a wee hauf yin. There was good Scots whisky there, but it was the tea I wanted. It was very hot in the sun, and I had done a deal of clambering about. So I was glad, after all, to stay in the shade a while and rest my limbs.

Getting out through Arras turned out to be a ticklish business. The Germans were verra wasteful o' their shells that day, considering how much siller they cost! They were pounding away, and more shells, by a good many, were falling in Arras than had been the case when we arrived at noon. So I got a chance to see how the ruin that had been wrought had been accomplished.

Arras is a wonderful sight, noble and impressive even in its destruction. But it was a sight that depressed me. It had angered me, at first, but now I began to think, at each ruined house that I saw: "Suppose this were at hame in Scotland!" And when such thoughts came to me I thanked God for the brave lads I had seen that day who stood, out here, holding the line, and so formed a bulwark between Scotland and such black ruin as this.

We were to start for Tramecourt now, but on the way we were to make a couple of stops. Our way was to take us through St. Pol and Hesdin, and, going so, we came to the town of Le Quesnoy. Here some of the 11th Argyle and Sutherland Highlanders were stationed. My heart leaped at the sight of them. That had been my boy's regiment, although he had belonged to a different battalion, and it was with the best will in the world that I called a halt and gave them a concert.

I gave two more concerts, both brief ones, on the rest of the journey, and so it was quite dark when we approached the château at Tramecourt. As we came up I became aware of a great stir and movement that was quite out of the ordinary routine there. In the grounds I could see tiny lights moving about, like fireflies – lights that came, I thought, from electric torches.

"Something extraordinary must be going on here," I remarked to Captain Godfrey. "I wonder if General Haig has arrived, by any chance?"

"We'll soon know what it's all about," he said, philosophically. But I expect he knew already.

Before the château there was a brilliant spot of light, standing out vividly against the surrounding darkness. I could not account for that brilliantly lighted spot then. But we came into it as the car stopped; it was a sort of oasis of light in an inky desert of surrounding gloom. And as we came full into it and I stood up to descend from the car, stretching my tired, stiff legs, the silence and the darkness were split by three tremendous cheers.

It wasn't General Haig who was arriving! It was Harry Lauder!

"What's the matter here?" I called, as loudly as I could.

"Been waitin' for ye a couple of 'ours, 'Arry," called a loud cockney voice in answer. "Go it now! Get it off your chest!" Then came explanations. It seemed that a lot of soldiers, about four hundred strong, who were working on a big road job about ten miles from Tramecourt, had heard of my being there, and had decided to come over in a body and beg for a concert. They got to the château early, and were told it might be eleven o'clock before I got back. But they didn't care – they said they'd wait all night, if they had to, to get a chance to hear me. And they made some use of the time they had to wait.

They took three big acetylene headlights from motor cars, and connected them up. There was a little porch at the entrance of the château, with a short flight of steps leading up to it, and then we decided that that would make an excellent makeshift theater. Since it would be dark they decided they must have lights, so that they could see me – just as in a regular theater at hame! That was where the headlights they borrowed from motor cars came in. They put one on each side of the porch and one off in front, so that all the light was centered right on the porch itself, and it was bathed in as strong a glare as ever I sang in on the stage. It was almost blinding, indeed, as I found when I turned to face them and to sing for them. Needless to say, late though it was and tired as I was, I never thought of refusing to give them the concert they wanted!

I should have liked to eat my dinner first, but I couldn't think of suggesting it. These boys had done a long, hard day's work. Then they had marched ten miles, and, on top of all that, had waited two hours for me and fixed up a stage and a lighting system. They were quite as tired as I, I decided – and they had done a lot more. And so I told the faithful Johnson to bring wee Tinkle Tom along, and get him up to the little stage, and I faced my audience in the midst of a storm of the ghostliest applause I ever hope to hear!

I could hear them, do you ken, but I could no see a face before me! In the theater, bright though the footlights are, and greatly as they dim what lies beyond them, you can still see the white faces of your audience. At least, you do see something – your eyes help you to know the audience is there, and, gradually, you can see perfectly, and pick out a face, maybe, and sing to some one person in the audience, that you may be sure of your effects.

It was utter, Stygian darkness that lay beyond the pool of blinding light in which I stood. Gradually I did make out a little of what lay beyond, very close to me. I could see dim outlines of human bodies moving around. And now I was sure there were fireflies about. But then they stayed so still that I realized, suddenly, with a smile, just what they were – the glowing ends of cigarettes, of course!

There were many tall poplar trees around the château. I knew where to look for them, but that night I could scarcely see them. I tried to find them, for it was a strange, weird sensation to be there as I was, and I wanted all the help fixed objects could give me. I managed to pick out their feathery lines in the black distance – the darkness made them seem more remote than they were, really. Their branches, when I found them, waved like spirit arms, and I could hear the wind whispering and sighing among the topmost branches.

Now and then what we call in Scotland a "batty bird" skimmed past my face, attracted, I suppose, by the bright light. I suppose that bats that have not been disturbed before for generations have been aroused by the blast of war through all that region and have come out of dark cavernous hiding-places, as those that night must have done, to see what it is all about, the tumult and the shouting!

They were verra disconcertin', those bats! They bothered me almost as much as the whizz bangs had done, earlier in the day! They swished suddenly out of the darkness against my face, and I would start back, and hear a ripple of laughter run through that unseen audience of mine. Aye, it was verra funny for them, but I did not like that part of it a bit! No man likes to have a bat touch his skin. And I had to duck quickly to evade those winged cousins of the mouse – and then hear a soft guffaw arising as I did it.

I have appeared, sometimes, in theaters in which it was pretty difficult to find the audience. And such audiences have been nearly impossible to trace, later, in the box-office reports. But that is the first time in my life, and, up to now, the last, that I ever sang to a totally invisible audience! I did not know then how many men there might have been forty, or four hundred, or four thousand. And, save for the titters that greeted my encounters with the bats, they were amazingly quiet as they waited for me to sing.

It was just about ten minutes before eleven when I began to sing, and the concert wasn't over until after midnight. I was distinctly nervous as I began the verse of my first song. It was a great relief when there was a round of applause; that helped to place my audience and give me its measure, at once.

But I was almost as disconcerted a bit later as I had been by the first incursion of the bats. I came to the chorus, and suddenly, out of the darkness, there came a perfect gale of sound. It was the men taking up the chorus, thundering it out. They took the song clean away from me – I could only gasp and listen. The roar from that unseen chorus almost took my feet from under me, so amazing was it, and so unexpected, somehow, used as I was to having soldiers join in a chorus with me, and disappointed as I should have been had they ever failed to do so.

But after that first song, when I knew what to expect, I soon grew used to the strange surroundings. The weirdness and the mystery wore off, and I began to enjoy myself tremendously. The conditions were simply ideal; indeed, they were perfect, for the sentimental songs that soldiers always like best. Imagine how "Roamin' in the Gloamin'" went that nicht!

I had meant to sing three or four songs. But instead I sang nearly every song I knew. It was one of the longest programmes I gave during the whole tour, and I enjoyed the concert, myself, better than any I had yet given.

My audience was growing all the time, although I did not know that. The singing brought up crowds from the French village, who gathered in the outskirts of the throng to listen – and, I make no doubt, to pass amazed comments on these queer English!

At last I was too tired to go on. And so I bade the lads good-nicht, and they gave me a great cheer, and faded away into the blackness. And I went inside, rubbing my eyes, and wondering if it was no all a dream!

"It wasn't Sir Douglas Haig who arrived, was it, Harry?" Godfrey said, slyly.

CHAPTER XXIV

The next morning I was tired, as you may believe. I ached in every limb when I went to my room that night, but a hot bath and a good sleep did wonders for me. No bombardment could have kept me awake that nicht! I would no ha' cared had the Hun begun shelling Tramecourt itself, so long as he did not shell me clear out of my bed.

Still, in the morning, though I had not had so much sleep as I would have liked, I was ready to go when we got the word. We made about as early a start as usual – breakfast soon after daylight, and then out the motor cars and to wee Tinkle Tom. Our destination that day, our first, at least, was Albert – a town as badly smashed and battered as Arras or Ypres. These towns were long thinly held by the British – that is, they were just within our lines, and the Hun could rake them with his fire at his own evil will.

It did him no good to batter them to pieces as he did. He wasted shells upon them that must have been precious to him. His treatment of them was but a part of his wicked, wanton spirit of destructiveness. He could not see a place standing that he did not want to destroy, I think. It was not war he made, as the world had known war; it was a savage raid against every sign and evidence of civilization, and comfort and happiness. But always, as I think I have said before, one thing eluded him. It was the soul of that which he destroyed. That was beyond his reach, and sore it must have grieved him to come to know it – for come to know it he has, in France, and in Belgium, too.

We passed through a wee town called Doullens on our way from Tramecourt to Albert. And there, that morn, I saw an old French nun; an aged woman, a woman old beyond all belief or reckoning. I think she is still there, where I saw her that day. Indeed, it has seemed to me, often, as I have thought upon her, that she will always be there, gliding silently through the deserted streets of that wee toon, on through all the ages that are to come, and always a cowled, veiled figure of reproach and hatred for the German race.

There is some life in that wee place now. There are no more Germans, and no more shells come there. The battle line has been carried on to the East by the British; here they have redeemed a bit of France from the German yoke. And so we could stop there, in the heat of the morning, for a bit of refreshment at a cafe that was once, I suppose, quite a place in that sma' toon. It does but little business now; passing soldiers bring it some trade, but nothing like what it used to have. For this is not a town much frequented by troops – or was not, just at that time.

There was some trouble, too, with one of the cars, so we went for a short walk through the town. It was then that we met that old French nun. Her face and her hands were withered, and deeply graven with the lines of the years that had bowed her head. Her back was bent, and she walked slowly and with difficulty. But in her eyes was a soft, young light that I have often seen in the eyes of priests and nuns, and that their comforting religion gives them. But as we talked I spoke of the Germans.

Gone from her eyes was all their softness. They flashed a bitter and contemptuous hatred.

"The Germans!" she said. She spat upon the ground, scornfully, and with a gesture of infinite loathing. And every time she uttered that hated word she spat again. It was a ceremony she used; she felt, I know, that her mouth was defiled by that word, and she wished to cleanse it. It was no affectation, as, with some folk, you might have thought it. It was not a studied act. She did it, I do believe, unconsciously. And it was a gesture marvelously expressive. It spoke more eloquently of her feelings than many words could have done.

She had seen the Germans! Aye! She had seen them come, in 1914, in the first days of the war, rolling past in great, gray waves, for days and days, as if the flood would never cease to roll. She had seen them passing, with their guns, in those first proud days of the war, when they had reckoned themselves invincible, and been so sure of victory. She knew what cruelties, what indignities, they had put upon the helpless people the war had swept into their clutch. She knew the defilements of which they had been guilty.

Nor was that the first time she had seen Germans. They had come before she was so old, though even then she had not been a young girl – in the war of 1870, when Europe left brave France to her fate, because the German spirit and the German plan were not appreciated or understood. Thank God the world had learned its lesson by 1914, when the Hun challenged it again, so that the challenge was met and taken up, and France was not left alone to bear the brunt of German greed and German hate.

She hated the Germans, that old French nun. She was religious; she knew the teachings of her church. She knew that God says we must love our enemies. But He could not expect us to love His enemies.

Albert, when we came to it, we found a ruin indeed. The German guns had beaten upon it until it was like a rubbish heap in the backyard of hell. Their malice had wrought a ruin here almost worse than that at Arras. Only one building had survived although it was crumbling to ruin. That was a church, and, as we approached it, we could see, from the great way off, a great gilded figure of the Holy Virgin, holding in her arms the infant Christ.

The figure leaned at such an angle, high up against the tottering wall of the church, that it seemed that it must fall at the next moment, even as we stared at it. But – it does not fall. Every breath of wind that comes sets it to swaying, gently. When the wind rises to a storm it must rock perilously indeed. But still it stays there, hanging like an inspiration straight from Heaven to all who see it. The peasants who gaze upon it each day in reverent awe whisper to you, if you ask them, that when it falls at last the war will be over, and France will be victorious.

That is rank superstition, you say? Aye, it may be! But in the region of the front everyone you meet has become superstitious, if that is the word you choose. That is especially true of the soldiers. Every man at the front, it seemed to me, was a fatalist. What is to be will be, they say. It is certain that this feeling has helped to make them indifferent to danger, almost, indeed, contemptuous of it. And in France, I was told, almost everywhere there were shrines in which figures of Christ or of His Mother had survived the most furious shelling. All the world knows, too, how, at Rheims, where the great Cathedral has been shattered in the wickedest and most wanton of all the crimes of that sort that the Germans have to their account, the statue of Jeanne d'Arc, who saved France long ago, stands untouched.

How is a man to account for such things as that? Is he to put them down to chance, to luck, to a blind fate? I, for one, cannot do so, nor will I try to learn to do it.

Fate, to be sure, is a strange thing, as my friends the soldiers know so well. But there is a difference between fate, or chance, and the sort of force that preserves statues like those I have named. A man never knows his luck; he does well not to brood upon it. I remember the case of a chap I knew, who was out for nearly three years, taking part in great battles from Mons to Arras. He was scratched once or twice, but was never even really wounded badly enough to go to hospital. He went to London, at last, on leave, and within an hour of the time when he stepped from his train at Charing Cross he was struck by a 'bus and killed. And there was the strange ease of my friend, Tamson, the baker, of which I told you earlier. No – a man never knows his fate!

So it seemed to me, as we drove toward Arras, and watched that mysterious figure, that God Himself had chosen to leave it there, as a sign and a warning and a promise all at once. There was no sign of life, at first, when we came into the town. Silence brooded over the ruins. We stopped to have a look around in that scene of desolation, and as the motors throbbed beneath the hoods it seemed to me the noise they made was close to being blasphemous. We were right under that hanging figure of the Virgin and of Christ, and to have left the silence unbroken would have been more seemly.

But it was not long before the silence of the town was broken by another sound. It was marching men we heard, but they were scuffling with their feet as they came; they had not the rhythmic tread of most of the British troops we had encountered. Nor were these men, when they swung into sight, coming around a pile of ruins, just like any British troops we had seen. I recognized them at once asAustralians – Kangaroos, as their mates in other divisions called them – by the way their campaign hats were looped up at one side. These were the first Australian troops I had seen since I had sailed from Sydney, in the early days of the war, nearly three years before. Three years! To think of it – and of what those years had seen!

"Here's a rare chance to give a concert!" I said, and held up my hand to the officer in command.

"Halt!" he cried, and then: "Stand at ease!" I was about to tell him why I had stopped them, and make myself known to them when I saw a grin rippling its way over all those bronzed faces – a grin of recognition. And

I saw that the officer knew me, too, even before a loud voice cried out:

"Good old Harry Lauder!"

That was a good Scots voice – even though its owner wore the Australian uniform.

"Would the boys like to hear a concert?" I asked the officer.

"That they would! By all means!" he said. "Glad of the chance! And so'm I! I've heard you just once before – in Sydney, away back in the summer of 1914."

Then the big fellow who had called my name spoke up again.

"Sing us 'Calligan,'" he begged. "Sing us 'Calligan,' Harry! I heard you sing it twenty-three years agone, in Motherwell Toon Hall!"

"Calligan!" The request for that song took me back indeed, through all the years that I have been before the public. It must have been at least twenty-three years since he had heard me sing that song – all of twenty-three years. "Calligan" had been one of the very earliest of my successes on the stage. I had not thought of the song, much less sung it, for years and years. In fact, though I racked my brains, I could not remember the words. And so, much as I should have liked to do so, I could not sing it for him. But if he was disappointed, he took it in good part, and he seemed to like some of the newer songs I had to sing for them as well as he could ever have liked old "Calligan."

I sang for these Kangaroos a song I had not sung before in France, because it seemed to be an especially auspicious time to try it. I wrote it while I was in Australia, with a view, particularly, to pleasing Australian audiences, and so repaying them, in some measure, for the kindly way in which they treated me while I was there. I call it "Australia Is the Land for Me," and this is the way it goes:

> There's a land I'd like to tell you all about
> It's a land in the far South Sea.
> It's a land where the sun shines nearly every day
> It's the land for you and me.
> It's the land for the man with the big strong arm
> It's the land for big hearts, too.
> It's a land we'll fight for, everything that's right for
> Australia is the real true blue!
>
> Refrain:
>
> It's the land where the sun shines nearly every day
> Where the skies are ever blue.
> Where the folks are as happy as the day is long
> And there's lots of work to do.
> Where the soft winds blow and the gum trees grow
> As far as the eye can see,
> Where the magpie chaffs and the cuckoo-burra laughs
> Australia is the land for me!

Those Kangaroos took to that song as a duck takes to water! They raised the chorus with me in a swelling roar as soon as they had heard it once, to learn it, and their voices roared through the ruins like vocal shrapnel. You could hear them whoop "Australia Is the Land for Me!" a mile away. And if anything could have brought down that tottering statue above us it would have been the way they sang. They put body and soul, as well as voice, into that final patriotic declaration of the song.

We had thought – I speak for Hogge and Adam and myself, and not for Godfrey, who did not have to think and guess, but know – we had thought, when we rolled into Albert, that it was a city of the dead, utterly deserted and forlorn. But now, as I went on singing, we found that that idea had been all wrong. For as the Australians whooped up their choruses other soldiers popped into sight. They came pouring from all directions.

I have seen few sights more amazing. They came from cracks and crevices, as it seemed; from under tumbled heaps of ruins, and dropping down from shells of houses where there were certainly no stairs. As I live, before I had finished my audience had been swollen to a great one of two thousand men! When they were all roaring out in a chorus you could scarce hear Johnson's wee piano at all – it sounded only like a feeble tinkle when there was a part for it alone.

I began shaking hands, when I had finished singing. That was a verrainjudeecious thing for me to attempt there! I had not reckoned with the strength of the grip of those laddies from the underside of the world. But I had been there, and I should have known.

Soon came the order to the Kangaroos: "Fall in!"

At once the habit of stern discipline prevailed. They swung off again, and the last we saw of them they were just brown men, disappearing along a brown road, bound for the trenches.

Swiftly the mole-like dwellers in Albert melted away, until only a few officers were left beside the members of the Reverend Harry Lauder, M.P., Tour. And I grew grave and distraught myself.

CHAPTER XXV

One of the officers at Albert was looking at me in a curiously intent fashion. I noticed that. And soon he came over to me. "Where do you go next, Harry?" he asked me. His voice was keenly sympathetic, and his eyes and his manner were very grave.

"To a place called Ovilliers," I said.

"So I thought," he said. He put out his hand, and I gripped it, hard. "I know, Harry. I know exactly where you are going, and I will send a man with you to act as your guide, who knows the spot you want to reach."

I couldn't answer him. I was too deeply moved. For Ovilliers is the spot where my son, Captain John Lauder, lies in his soldier's grave. That grave had been, of course, from the very first, the final, the ultimate objective of my journey. And that morning, as we set out from Tramecourt, Captain Godfrey had told me, with grave sympathy, that at last we were coming to the spot that had been so constantly in my thoughts ever since we had sailed from Folkestone.

And so a private soldier joined our party as guide, and we took to the road again. The Bapaume road it was – a famous highway, bitterly contested, savagely fought for. It was one of the strategic roads of that whole region, and the Hun had made a desperate fight to keep control of it. But he had failed – as he has failed, and is failing still, in all his major efforts in France.

There was no talking in our car, which, this morning, was the second in the line. I certainly was not disposed to chat, and I suppose that sympathy for my feelings, and my glumness, stilled the tongues of my companions. And, at any rate, we had not traveled far when the car ahead of us stopped, and the soldier from Albert stepped into the road and waited for me. I got out when our car stopped, and joined him.

"I will show you the place now, Mr. Lauder," he said, quietly. So we left the cars standing in the road, and set out across a field that, like all the fields in that vicinity, had been ripped and torn by shell-fire. All about us, as we crossed that tragic field, there were little brown mounds, each with a white wooden cross upon it. June was out that day in full bloom. All over the valley, thickly sown with those white crosses, wild flowers in rare profusion, and thickly matted, luxuriant grasses, and all the little shrubs that God Himself looks after were growing bravely in the sunlight, as though they were trying to hide the work of the Hun.

It was a mournful journey, but, in some strange way, the peaceful beauty of the day brought comfort to me.

And my own grief was altered by the vision of the grief that had come to so many others. Those crosses, stretching away as far as my eye could reach, attested to the fact that it was not I alone who had suffered and lost and laid a sacrifice upon the altar of my country. And, in the presence of so many evidences of grief and desolation a private grief sank into its true proportions. It was no less keen, the agony of the thought of my boy was as sharp as ever. But I knew that he was only one, and that I was only one father. And there were so many like him – and so many like me, God help us all! Well, He did help me, as I have told, and I hope and pray that He has helped many another. I believe He has; indeed, I know it.

Hogge and Dr. Adam, my two good friends, walked with me on that sad pilgrimage. I was acutely conscious of their sympathy; it was sweet and precious to have it. But I do not think we exchanged a word as we crossed that field. There was no need of words. I knew, without speech from them, how they felt, and they knew that I knew. So we came, when we were, perhaps, half a mile from the Bapaume road, to a slight eminence, a tiny hill that rose from the field. A little military cemetery crowned it. Here the graves were set in ordered rows, and there was a fence set around them, to keep them apart, and to mark that spot as holy ground, until the end of time. Five hundred British boys lie sleeping in that small acre of silence, and among them is my own laddie. There the fondest hopes of my life, the hopes that sustained and cheered me through many years, lie buried.

No one spoke. But the soldier pointed, silently and eloquently, to one brown mound in a row of brown mounds that looked alike, each like the other. Then he drew away. And Hogge and Adam stopped, and stood together, quiet and grave. And so I went alone to my boy's grave, and flung myself down upon the warm, friendly earth. My memories of that moment are not very clear, but I think that for a few minutes I was utterly spent, that my collapse was complete.

He was such a good boy!

I hope you will not think, those of you, my friends, who may read what I am writing here, that I am exalting my lad above all the other Britons who died for King and country – or, and aye, above the brave laddies of other races who died to stop the Hun. But he was such a good boy!

As I lay there on that brown mound, under the June sun that day, all that he had been, and all that he had meant to me and to his mother came rushing back afresh to my memory, opening anew my wounds of grief. I thought of him as a baby, and as a wee laddie beginning to run around and talk to us. I thought of him in every phase and bit of his life, and of the friends that we had been, he and I! Such chums we were, always!

And as I lay there, as I look back upon it now, I can think of but the one desire that ruled and moved me. I wanted to reach my arms down into that dark grave, and clasp my boy tightly to my breast, and kiss him. And I wanted to thank him for what he had done for his country, and his mother, and for me.

Again there came to me, as I lay there, the same gracious solace that God had given me after I heard of his glorious death. And I knew that this dark grave, so sad and lonely and forlorn, was but the temporary bivouac of my boy. I knew that it was no more than a trench of refuge against the storm of battle, in which he was resting until that hour shall sound when we shall all be reunited beyond the shadowy borderland of Death.

How long did I lie there? I do not know. And how I found the strength at last to drag myself to my feet and away from that spot, the dearest and the saddest spot on earth to me, God only knows. It was an hour of very great anguish for me; an hour of an anguish different, but only less keen, than that which I had known when they had told me first that I should never see my laddie in the flesh again. But as I took up the melancholy journey across that field, with its brown mounds and its white crosses stretching so far away, they seemed to bring me a sort of tragic consolation.

I thought of all the broken-hearted ones at home, in Britain. How many were waiting, as I had waited, until they, too, – they, too, – might come to France, and cast themselves down, as I had done, upon some brown mound, sacred in their thoughts? How many were praying for the day to come when they might gaze upon a white cross, as I had done, and from the brown mound out of which it rose gather a few crumbs of that brown earth, to be deposited in a sacred corner of a sacred place yonder in Britain?

While I was in America, on my last tour, a woman wrote to me from a town in the state of Maine. She was a stranger to me when she sat down to write that letter, but I count her now, although I have never seen her, among my very dearest friends.

"I have a friend in France," she wrote. "He is there with our American army, and we had a letter from him the other day. I think you would like to hear what he wrote to us.

"'I was walking in the gloaming here in France the other evening,' he wrote. 'You know, I have always been very fond of that old song of Harry Lauder's, "Roamin' in the Gloamin'."'

"'Well, I was roamin' in the gloamin' myself, and as I went I hummed that very song, under my breath. And I came, in my walk to a little cemetery, on a tiny hill. There were many mounds there and many small white crosses. About one of them a Union Jack was wrapped so tightly that I could not read the inscription upon it. And something led me to unfurl that weather-worn flag, so that I could read. And what do you think? It was the grave of Harry Lauder's son, Captain John Lauder, of the Argyle and Sutherland Highlanders, and his little family crest was upon the cross.

"'I stood there, looking down at that grave, and I said a little prayer, all by myself. And then I rewound the Union Jack about the cross. I went over to some ruins nearby, and there I found a red rose growing. I do believe it was the last rose of summer. And I took it up, very carefully, roots and all, and carried it over to Captain Lauder's grave, and planted it there.'"

What a world of comfort those words brought me!

It was about eight o'clock one morning that Captain Lauder was killed, between Courcellete and Poiziéres, on the Ancre, in the region that is known as the Somme battlefield. It was soon after breakfast, and John was going about, seeing to his men. His company was to be relieved that day, and to go back from the trenches to rest billets, behind the lines. We had sent our laddie a braw lot of Christmas packages not long before, but he had had them kept at the rest billet, so that he might have the pleasure of opening them when he was out of the trenches, and had a little leisure, even though it made his Christmas presents a wee bit late.

There had been a little mist upon the ground, as, at that damp and chilly season of the year, there nearly always was along the river Ancre. At that time, on that morning, it was just beginning to rise as the sun grew strong enough to banish it. I think John trusted too much to the mist, perhaps. He stepped for just a moment into the open; for just a moment he exposed himself, as he had to do, no doubt, to do his duty. And a German sniper, watching for just such chances, caught a glimpse of him. His rifle spoke; its bullet pierced John's brave and gentle heart.

Tate, John's body-servant, a man from our own town, was the first to reach him. Tate was never far from John's side, and he was heart-broken when he reached him that morning and found that there was nothing he could do for him.

Many of the soldiers who served with John and under him have written to me, and come to me. And all of them have told me the same thing: that there was not a man in his company who did not feel his death as a personal loss and bereavement. And his superior officers have told me the same thing. In so far as such reports could comfort us his mother and I have taken solace in them. All that we have heard of John's life in the trenches, and of his death, was such a report as we or any parents should want to have of their boy.

John never lost his rare good nature. There were times when things were going very badly indeed, but at such times he could always be counted upon to raise a laugh and uplift the spirits of his men. He knew them all; he knew them well. Nearly all of them came from his home region near the Clyde, and so they were his neighbors and his friends.

I have told you earlier that John was a good musician. He played the piano rarely well, for an amateur, and he had a grand singing voice. And one of his fellow-officers told me that, after the fight at Beaumont-Hamul, one of the phases of the great Battle of the Somme, John's company found itself, toward evening, near the ruins of an old château. After that fight, by the way, dire news, sad news, came to our village of the men of the Argyle and Sutherland regiment, and there were many stricken homes that mourned brave lads who would never come home again.

John's men were near to exhaustion that night. They had done terrible work that day, and their losses had been heavy. Now that there was an interlude they lay about, tired and bruised and battered. Many had been killed; many had been so badly wounded that they lay somewhere behind, or had been picked up already by the Red Cross men who followed them across the field of the attack. But there were many more who had been slightly hurt, and whose wounds began to pain them grievously now. The spirit of the men was dashed.

John's friend and fellow-officer told me of the scene.

"There we were, sir," he said. "We were pretty well done in, I can tell you. And then Lauder came along. I suppose he was just as tired and worn out as the rest of us – God knows he had as much reason to be, and more! But he was as cocky as a little bantam. And he was smiling. He looked about.

"'Here – this won't do!' he said. 'We've got to get these lads feeling better!' He was talking more to himself than to anyone else, I think. And he went exploring around. He got into what was left of that château – and I can tell you it wasn't much! The Germans had been using it as a point d'appui – a sort of rallying-place, sir – and our guns had smashed it up pretty thoroughly. I've no doubt the Fritzies had taken a hack at it, too, when they found they couldn't hold it any longer – they usually did.

"But, by a sort of miracle, there was a piano inside that had come through all the trouble. The building and all the rest of the furniture had been knocked to bits, but the piano was all right, although, as I say, I don't know how that had happened. Lauder spied it, and went clambering over all the debris and wreckage to reach it. He tried the keys, and found that the action was all right. So he began picking out a tune, and the rest of us began to sit up a bit. And pretty soon he lifted his voice in a rollicking tune – one of your songs it was, sir – and in no time the men were all sitting up to listen to him. Then they joined in the chorus – and pretty soon you'd never have known they'd been tired or worn out! If there'd been a chance they'd have gone at Fritz and done the day's work all over again!"

After John was killed his brother officers sent us all his personal belongings. We have his field-glasses, with the mud of the trenches dried upon them. We have a little gold locket that he always wore around his neck. His mother's picture is in it, and that of the lassie he was to have married had he come home, after New Year's. And we have his rings, and his boots, and his watch, and all the other small possessions that were a part of his daily life out there in France.

Many soldiers and officers of the Argyle and Sutherlanders pass the hoose at Dunoon on the Clyde. None ever passes the hoose, though, without dropping in, for a bite and sup if he has time to stop, and to tell us stories of our beloved boy.

No, I would no have you think that I would exalt my boy above all the others who have lived and died in France in the way of duty. But he was such a good boy! We have heard so many tales like those I have told you, to make us proud of him, and glad that he bore his part as a man should.

He will stay there, in that small grave on that tiny hill. I shall not bring his body back to rest in Scotland, even if the time comes when I might do so. It is a soldier's grave, and an honorable place for him to be, and I feel it is there that he would wish to lie, with his men lying close about him, until the time comes for the great reunion.

But I am going back to France to visit again and again that grave where he lies buried. So long as I live myself that hill will be the shrine to which my many pilgrimages will be directed. The time will come again when I may take his mother with me, and when we may kneel together at that spot.

And meanwhile the wild flowers and the long grasses and all the little shrubs will keep watch and ward over him there, and over all the other brave soldiers who lie hard by, who died for God and for their flag.

CHAPTER XXVI

So at last, I turned back toward the road, and very slowly, with bowed head and shoulders that felt very old, all at once, I walked back toward the Bapaume highway. I was still silent, and when we reached the road again, and the waiting cars, I turned, and looked back, long and sorrowfully, at that tiny hill, and the grave it sheltered. Godfrey and Hogge and Adam, Johnson and the soldiers of our party, followed my gaze. But we looked in silence; not one of us had a word to say. There are moments, as I suppose we have all had to learn, that are beyond words and speech.

And then at last we stepped back into the cars, and resumed our journey on the Bapaume road. We started slowly, and I looked back until a turn in the road hid that field with its mounds and its crosses, and that tiny cemetery on the wee hill. So I said good-by to my boy again, for a little space.

Our road was by way of Poizieres, and this part of our journey took us through an area of fearful desolation. It was the country that was most bitterly fought over in the summer long battle of the Somme in 1916, when the new armies of Britain had their baptism of fire and sounded the knell of doom for the Hun. It was then he learned that Britain had had time, after all, to train troops who, man for man, outmatched his best.

Here war had passed like a consuming flame, leaving no living thing in its path. The trees were mown down, clean to the ground. The very earth was blasted out of all semblance to its normal kindly look. The scene was like a picture of Hell from Dante's Inferno; there is nothing upon this earth that may be compared with it. Death and pain and agony had ruled this whole countryside, once so smiling and fair to see.

After we had driven for a space we came to something that lay by the roadside that was a fitting occupant of such a spot. It was like the skeleton of some giant creature of a prehistoric age, incredibly savage even in its stark, unlovely death. It might have been the frame of some vast, metallic tumble bug, that, crawling ominously along this road of death, had come into the path of a Colossus, and been stepped upon, and then kicked aside from the road to die.

"That's what's left of one of our first tanks," said Godfrey. "We used them first in this battle of the Somme, you remember. And that must have been one of the very earliest ones. They've been improved and perfected since that time."

"How came it like this?" I asked, gazing at it, curiously.

"A direct hit from a big German shell – a lucky hit, of course. That's about the only thing that could put even one of the first tanks out of action that way. Ordinary shells from field pieces, machine-gun fire, that sort of thing, made no impression on the tanks. But, of course —."

I could see for myself. The in'ards of the monster had been pretty thoroughly knocked out. Well, that tank had done its bit, I have no doubt. And, since its heyday, the brain of Mars has spawned so many new ideas that this vast creature would have been obsolete, and ready for the scrap heap, even had the Hun not put it there before its time.

At the Butte de Marlincourt, one of the most bitterly contested bits of the battlefield, we passed a huge mine crater, and I made an inspection of it. It was like the crater of an old volcano, a huge old mountain with a hole in its center. Here were elaborate dugouts, too, and many graves.

Soon we came to Bapaume. Bapaume was one of the objectives the British failed to reach in the action of 1916. But early in 1917 the Germans, seeing they had come to the end of their tether there, retreated, and gave the town up. But what a town they left! Bapaume was nearly as complete a ruin as Arras and Albert. But it had not been wrecked by shell-fire. The Hun had done the work in cold blood. The houses had been wrecked by human hands. Pictures still hung crazily upon the walls. Grates were falling out of fire-places. Beds stood on end. Tables and chairs were wantonly smashed and there was black ruin everywhere.

We drove on then to a small town where the skirling of pipes heralded our coming. It was the headquarters of General Willoughby and the Fortieth Division. Highlanders came flocking around to greet us warmly, and they all begged me to sing to them. But the officer in command called them to attention.

"Men," he said, "Harry Lauder comes to us fresh from the saddest mission of his life. We have no right to expect him to sing for us to-day, but if it is God's will that he should, nothing could give us greater pleasure."

My heart was very heavy within me, and never, even on the night when I went back to the Shaftesbury Theater, have I felt less like singing. But I saw the warm sympathy on the faces of the boys.

"If you'll take me as I am," I told them, "I will try to sing for you. I will do my best, anyway. When a man is killed, or a battalion is killed, or a regiment is killed, the war goes on, just the same. And if it is possible for you to fight with broken ranks, I'll try to sing for you with a broken heart."

And so I did, and, although God knows it must have been a feeble effort, the lads gave me a beautiful reception. I sang my older songs for them – the songs my own laddie had loved.

They gave us tea after I had sung for them, with chocolate eclairs as a rare treat! We were surprised to get such fare upon the battlefield, but it was a welcome surprise.

We turned back from Bapaume, traveling along another road on the return journey. And on the way we met about two hundred German prisoners – the first we had seen in any numbers. They were working on the road, under guard of British soldiers. They looked sleek and well-fed, and they were not working very hard, certainly. Yet I thought there was something about their expression like that of neglected animals. I got out of the car and spoke to an intelligent- looking little chap, perhaps about twenty-five years old – a sergeant. He looked rather suspicious when I spoke to him, but he saluted smartly, and stood at attention while we talked, and he gave me ready and civil answers.

"You speak English?" I asked. "Fluently?"

"Yes, sir!"

"How do you like being a prisoner?"

"I don't like it. It's very degrading."

"Your companions look pretty happy. Any complaints?"

"No, sir! None!"

"What are the Germans fighting for? What do you hope to gain?"

"The freedom of the seas!"

"But you had that before the war broke out!"

"We haven't got it now."

I laughed at that.

"Certainly not," I said. "Give us credit for doing something! But how are you going to get it again?"

"Our submarines will get it for us."

"Still," I said, "you must be fighting for something else, too?"

"No," he said, doggedly. "Just for the freedom of the seas."

I couldn't resist telling him a bit of news that the censor was keeping very carefully from his fellow-Germans at home.

"We sank seven of your submarines last week," I said.

He probably didn't believe that. But his face paled a bit, and his lips puckered, and he scowled. Then, as I turned away, he whipped his hand to his forehead in a stiff salute, but I felt that it was not the most gracious salute I had ever seen! Still, I didn't blame him much!

Captain Godfrey meant to show us another village that day.

"Rather an interesting spot," he said. "They differ, these French villages. They're not all alike, by any means."

Then, before long, he began to look puzzled. And finally he called a halt.

"It ought to be right here," he said. "It was, not so long ago."

But there was no village! The Hun had passed that way. And the village for which Godfrey was seeking had been utterly wiped off the face of the earth! Not a trace of it remained. Where men and women and little children had lived and worked and played in quiet happiness the abominable desolation that is the work of the Hun had come. There was nothing to show that they or their village had ever been.

The Hun knows no mercy!

CHAPTER XXVII

There had been, originally, a perfectly definite route for the Reverend Harry Lauder, M.P., Tour – as definite a route as is mapped out for me when I am touring the United States. Our route had called for a fairly steady progress from Vimy Ridge to Peronne – like Bapaume, one of the great unreached objectives of the Somme offensive, and, again like Bapaume, ruined and abandoned by the Germans in the retreat of the spring of 1917. But we made many side trips and gave many and many an unplanned, extemporaneous roadside concert, as I have told.

For all of us it had been a labor of love. I will always believe that I sang a little better on that tour than I have ever sung before or ever shall again, and I am sure, too, that Hogge and Dr. Adam spoke more eloquently to their soldier hearers than they ever did in parliament or church. My wee piano, Tinkle Tom, held out staunchly. He never wavered in tune, though he got some sad jouncings as he clung to the grid of a swift-moving car. As for Johnson, my Yorkshireman, he was as good an accompanist before the tour ended as I could ever want, and he took the keenest interest and delight in his work, from start to finish.

Captain Godfrey, our manager, must have been proud indeed of the "business" his troupe did. The weather was splendid; the "houses" everywhere were so big that if there had been Standing Room Only signs they would have been called into use every day. And his company got a wonderful reception wherever it showed! He had everything a manager could have to make his heart rejoice. And he did not, like many managers, have to be continually trying to patch up quarrels in the company! He had no petty professional jealousies with which to contend; such things were unknown in our troupe!

All the time while I was singing in France I was elaborating an idea that had for some time possessed me, and that was coming now to dominate me utterly. I was thinking of the maimed soldiers, the boys who had not died, but had given a leg, or an arm, or their sight to the cause, and who were doomed to go through the rest of their lives broken and shattered and incomplete. They were never out of my thoughts. I had seen them before I ever came to France, as I traveled the length and breadth of the United Kingdom, singing for the men in the camps and the hospitals, and doing what I could to help in the recruiting. And I used to lie awake of nights, wondering what would become of those poor broken laddies when the war was over and we were all setting to work again to rebuild our lives.

And especially I thought of the brave laddies of my ain Scotland. They must have thought often of their future. They must have wondered what was to become of them, when they had to take up the struggle with the world anew – no longer on even terms with their mates, but handicapped by grievous injuries that had come to them in the noblest of ways. I remembered crippled soldiers, victims of other wars, whom I had seen selling papers and matches on street corners, objects of charity, almost, to a generation that had forgotten the service to the country that had put them in the way of having to make their living so. And I had made a great resolution that, if I could do aught to prevent it, no man of Scotland who had served in this war should ever have to seek a livelihood in such a manner.

So I conceived the idea of raising a great fund to be used for giving the maimed Scots soldiers a fresh start in life. They would be pensioned by the government. I knew that. But I knew, too, that a pension is rarely more than enough to keep body and soul together. What these crippled men would need, I felt, was enough money to set them up in some little business of their own, that they could see to despite their wounds, or to enable them to make a new start in some old business or trade, if they could do so.

A man might need a hundred pounds, I thought, or two hundred pounds, to get him started properly again. And I wanted to be able to hand a man what money he might require. I did not want to lend it to him, taking his note or his promise to pay. Nor did I want to give it to him as charity. I wanted to hand it to him as a freewill offering, as a partial payment of the debt Scotland owed him for what he had done for her.

And I thought, too, of men stricken by shell-shock, or paralyzed in the war – there are pitifully many of both sorts! I did not want them to stay in bare and cold and lonely institutions. I wanted to take them out of such places, and back to their homes; home to the village and the glen. I wanted to get them a wheel-chair, with an old, neighborly man or an old neighborly woman, maybe, to take them for an airing in the forenoon, and the afternoon, that they might breathe the good Scots air, and see the wild flowers growing, and hear the song of the birds.

That was the plan that had for a long time been taking form in my mind. I had talked it over with some of my friends, and the newspapers had heard of it, somehow, and printed a few paragraphs about it. It was still very much in embryo when I went to France, but, to my surprise, the Scots soldiers nearly always spoke of it when I was talking with them. They had seen the paragraphs in the papers, and I soon realized that it loomed up as a great thing for them.

"Aye, it's a grand thing you're thinking of, Harry," they said, again and again. "Now we know we'll no be beggars in the street, now that we've got a champion like you, Harry."

I heard such words as that first from a Highlander at Arras, and from that moment I have thought of little else. Many of the laddies told me that the thought of being killed did not bother them, but that they did worry a bit about their future in case they went home maimed and helpless.

"We're here to stay until there's no more work to do, if it takes twenty years, Harry," they said. "But it'll be a big relief to know we will be cared for if we must go back crippled."

I set the sum I would have to raise to accomplish the work I had in mind at a million pounds sterling – five million dollars. It may seem a great sum to some, but to me, knowing the purpose for which it is to be used, it seems small enough. And my friends agree with me. When I returned from France I talked to some Scots friends, and a meeting was called, in Glasgow, of the St. Andrews Society. I addressed it, and it declared itself in cordial sympathy with the idea. Then I went to Edinburgh, and down to London, and back north to Manchester. Everywhere my plan was greeted with the greatest enthusiasm, and the real organization of the fund was begun on September 17 and 18, 1917.

This fund of mine is known officially as "The Harry Lauder Million Pound Fund for Maimed Men, Scottish Soldiers and Sailors." It does not in any way conflict with nor overlap, any other work already being done. I made sure of that, because I talked to the Pension Minister, and his colleagues, in London, before I went ahead with my plans, and they fully and warmly approved everything that I planned to do.

The Earl of Rosebery, former Prime Minister of Britain, is Honorary President of the Fund, and Lord Balfour of Burleigh is its treasurer. And as I write we have raised an amount well into six figures in pounds sterling. One of the things that made me most willing to undertake my last tour of America was my feeling that I could secure the support and cooperation of the Scottish people in America for my fund better by personal appeals than in any other way. At the end of every performance I gave during the tour, I told my audience what I was doing and the object of the fund, and, although I addressed myself chiefly to the Scots, there has been a most generous and touching response from Americans as well.

We distributed little plaid-bordered envelopes, in which folk were invited to send contributions to the bank in New York that was the American depository. And after each performance Mrs. Lauder stood in the lobby and sold little envelopes full of stamps, "sticky backs," as she called them, like the Red Cross seals that have been sold so long in America at Christmas time. She sold them for a quarter, or for whatever they would bring, and all the money went to the fund.

I had a novel experience sometimes. Often I would no sooner have explained what I was doing than I would feel myself the target of a sort of bombardment. At first I thought Germans were shooting at me, but I soon learned that it was money that was being thrown! And every day my dressing-table would be piled high with checks and money orders and paper money sent direct to me instead of to the bank. But I had to ask the guid folk to cease firing – the money was too apt to be lost!

Folk of all races gave liberally. I was deeply touched at Hot Springs, Arkansas, where the stage hands gave me the money they had received for their work during my engagement.

CHAPTER XXVIII

I have stopped for a wee digression about my fund. I saw many interesting things in France, and dreadful things. And it was impressed upon me more and more that the Hun knows no mercy. The wicked, wanton things he did in France, and that I saw!

There was Mont St. Quentin, one of the very strongest of the positions out of which the British turned him. There was a château there, a bonnie place. And hard by was a wee cemetery. The Hun had smashed its pretty monuments, and he had reached into that sacred soil with his filthy claws, and dragged out the dead from their resting-place, and scattered their helpless bones about.

He ruined Peronne in wanton fury because it was passing from his grip. He wrecked its old cathedral, once one of the loveliest sights in France. He took away the old fleurs-de-lis from the great gates of Peronne. He stole and carried away the statues that used to stand in the old square. He left the great statue of St. Peter, still standing in the churchyard, but its thumb was broken off. I found it, as I rummaged about idly in the debris at the statue's foot.

It was no casual looting that the Huns did. They did their work methodically, systematically. It was a sight to make the angels weep.

As I left the ruined cathedral I met a couple of French poilus, and tried to talk with them. But they spoke "very leetle" English, and I fired all my French words at them in one sentence.

"Oui, oui, madame," I said. "Encore pomme du terre. Fini!"

They laughed, but we did no get far with our talk! Not in French.

"You can't love the Hun much, after this," I said.

"Ze Hun? Ze bloody Boche?" cried one of them. "I keel heem all my life!"

I was glad to quit Peronne. The rape of that lovely church saddened me more than almost any sight I saw in France. I did not care to look at it. So I was glad when we motored on to the headquarters of the Fourth Army, where I had the honor of meeting one of Britain's greatest soldiers, General Sir Henry Rawlinson, who greeted us most cordially, and invited us to dinner.

After dinner we drove on toward Amiens. We were swinging back now, toward Boulogne, and were scheduled to sleep that night at Amiens – which the Germans held for a few days, during their first rush toward Paris, before the Marne, but did not have time to destroy.

Adam knew Amiens, and was made welcome, with the rest of us, at an excellent hotel. Von Kluck had made its headquarters when he swung that way from Brussels, and it was there he planned the dinner he meant to eat in Paris with the Kaiser. Von Kluck demanded an indemnity of a million dollars from Amiens to spare its famous old cathedral.

It was late when we arrived, but before I slept I called for the boots and ordered a bottle of ginger ale. I tried to get him to tell me about old von Kluck and his stay but he couldn't talk English, and was busy, anyway, trying to open the bottle without cutting the wire. Adam and Hogge are fond, to this day, of telling how I shouted at him, finally:

"Well, how do you expect to open that bottle when you can't even talk the English language?"

Next day was Sunday, and we went to church in the cathedral, which von Kluck didn't destroy, after all. There were signs of war; the windows and the fine carved doors were banked with sand bags as a measure of protection from bombing airplanes.

I gave my last roadside concert on the road from Amiens to Boulogne. It was at a little place called Ouef, and we had some trouble in finding it and more in pronouncing its name. Some of us called it Off, some Owf! I knew I had heard the name somewhere, and I was racking my brains to think as Johnson set up our wee piano and I began to sing. Just as I finished my first song a rooster set up a violent crowing, in competition with me, and I remembered!

"I know where I am!" I cried. "I'm at Egg!"

And that is what Oeuf means, in English!

The soldiers were vastly amused. They were Gordon Highlanders, and I found a lot of chaps among them frae far awa' Aberdeen. Not many of them are alive to-day! But that day they were a gay lot and a bonnie lot. There was a big Highlander who said to me, very gravely:

"Harry, the only good thing I ever saw in a German was a British bayonet! If you ever hear anyone at hame talking peace – cut off their heads! Or send them out to us, and we'll show them. There's a job to do here, and we'll do it.

"Look!" he said, sweeping his arm as if to include all France. "Look at yon ruins! How would you like old England or auld Scotland to be looking like that? We're not only going to break and scatter the Hun rule, Harry. If we do no more than that, it will surely be reassembled again. We're going to destroy it."

On the way from Oeuf to Boulogne we visited a small, out of the way hospital, and I sang for the lads there. And I was going around, afterward, talking to the boys on their cots, and came to a young chap whose head and face were swathed in bandages.

"How came you to be hurt, lad?" I asked.

"Well, sir," he said, "we were attacking one morning. I went over the parapet with the rest, and got to the German trench all right. I wasn't hurt. And I went down, thirty feet deep, into one of their dugouts. You wouldn't think men could live so – but, of course, they're not men – they're animals! There was a lighted candle on a shelf, and beside it a fountain pen. It was just an ordinary-looking pen, and it was fair loot – I thought some chap had meant to write a letter, and forgotten his pen when our attack came. So I slipped it in my pocket.

"Two days later I was going to write a few lines to my mother and tell her I was all right, so I thought I'd try my new pen. And when I unscrewed the cap it exploded – and, well, you see me, Harry! It blew half of my face away!"

The Hun knows no mercy.

I was glad to see Boulogne again – the white buildings on the white hills, and the harbor beyond. Here the itinerary of the Reverend Harry Lauder, M.P., Tour, came to its formal end. But, since there were many new arrivals in the hospitals – the population of a base shifts quickly – we were asked to give a couple more concerts in the hospitals where we had first appeared on French soil.

A good many thousand Canadians had just come in, so I sang at Base Hospital No. 1, and then gave another and farewell concert at the great convalescent camp on the hill. And then we said good-by to Captain Godfrey, and the chauffeurs, and to Johnson, my accompanist, ready to go back to his regiment now. I told them all I hoped that when I came to France again to sing we could reassemble all the original cast, and I pray that we may!

On Monday we took the boat again for Folkestone. The boat was crowded with men going home on leave, and I wandered among them. I heard many a tale of heroism and courage, of splendid sacrifice and suffering nobly borne. Destroyers, as before, circled about us, and there was no hint of trouble from a Hun submarine.

On our boat was Lord Dalmeny, a King's Messenger, carrying dispatches from the front. He asked me how I had liked the "show." It is so that nearly all British soldiers refer to the war.

They had earned their rest, those laddies who were going home to Britain. But some of them were half sorry to be going! I talked to one of them.

ABOUT THE AUTHOR

Harry Lauder was born in Scotland in 1870. He toured the world as a singer and performer for 40 years. He was the first British entertainer to sell a million records and was knighted in 1919 by King George V. He wrote most of his own songs, including "Roamin' in the Gloamin'," "I Love a Lassie," and "Keep Right on to the End of the Road," the last in memory of his son John. He also wrote several books and starred in popular films. He continued to entertain the troops in World War II, publicly thanking the Americans who brought food to Britain in her hour of need. Sir Harry Lauder passed away in 1950, having lived a full and adventure-filled life.

HISTORICAL MEMOIRS FROM 1500 BOOKS

The Private Life of Marie Antoinette by Madame Campan – An intimate account of the intrigue and drama of the royal court from the Queen's trusted Lady-in-Waiting. (September 2006)

A Minstrel In France by Harry Lauder – A world famous performer's life is forever changed by the loss of his beloved son in World War I. With a piano lashed to his jeep Lauder tours the battlefront in France paying tribute to the troops. (October 2006)

A Year With A Whaler by Walter Noble Burns – The stories of the able-bodied seamen, the great mammals, and the ever changing sea are the central figures in this narrative of a carefree boy shipping out and a wise man returning. (November 2006)

Thirty Years A Detective by Allan Pinkerton – From the founder of the Pinkerton agency an insider's look at criminals, their mindsets, and their most famous schemes. (December 2006)

A New Voyage Round the World by William Dampier – A fascinating travelogue, a scientific journey, and a buccaneering adventure from Dampier – gentleman sailor and pirate. (January 2007)

The Arctic Prairies by Ernest Thompson Seton – Two naturalists travel two thousand miles of river by canoe in search of caribou. A true adventure from an early environmentalist. (February 2007)

The Life and Times of Frederick Reynolds by Himself – A noted 18th century dramatist's account of life behind the theater curtain from staging a play to managing the celebrities to making a living. (March 2007)

To Cuba and Back by Richard Henry Dana – The best-selling author's account of his 1859 trip to the tropical island where colonial expansionism and slavery meet head on. (March 2007)

Excerpt from

A YEAR WITH A
WHALER

by

WALTER NOBLE BURNS

to be published by 1500 Books
in November 2006

CHAPTER XI

WE had hardly washed clear of the ice in the heavy seas when "Blow!" rang from the crow's nest. A school of whales close ahead, covering the sea with fountains, was coming leisurely toward the ship. There were more than thirty of them.

"Bowheads!" shouted the mate.

Their great black heads rose above the surface like ponderous pieces of machinery; tall fountains shot into the air; the wind caught the tops of the fountains and whisked them off in smoke; hollow, sepulchral whispers of sound came to the brig as the breath left the giant lungs in mighty exhalations. Why they were called bowheads was instantly apparent—the outline of the top of the head curved like an Indian's bow. As the head sank beneath the surface, the glistening back, half as broad as a city street and as black as asphalt, came spinning up out of the sea and went spinning down again.

Our crippled captain in his fur clothes and on crutches limped excitedly about the quarter-deck glaring at $300,000 worth of whales spouting under his nose. But with so much ice about and such a heavy sea running he was afraid to lower.

If the whales saw the brig they gave no sign. They passed all around the vessel, the spray of their fountains blowing on deck. One headed straight for the ship. The mate seized a shoulder bomb-gun and ran to the bow. The whale rose, blew a fountain up against the jib-boom, and dived directly beneath the brig's forefoot. As its back curled down, the mate, with one knee resting on the starboard knighthead, took aim and fired. He surely hit the whale—there was little chance to miss. But the bomb evidently did not strike a vital spot, for the leviathan passed under the ship, came up on the other side and went on about its business.

The sight of all these whales passing by us with such unconcern, blowing water on us as if in huge contempt, almost seeming to laugh at us and mock our bombs and harpoons and human skill, drove the captain frantic. Should he allow that fortune in whales to escape him without a try for it? With purple face and popping eyes he gazed at the herd now passing astern.

"Lower them boats!" he cried.

"What?" expostulated Mr. Landers. "Do you want to get us all killed?"

"Lower them boats!" yelled the skipper.

"Don't you know that a boat that gets fast to a whale in that ice will be smashed, sure?"

"Lower them boats!" shouted the captain.

Mr. Winchester, enthusiastic and fearless whaleman that he was, was eager for the captain's order. His boat and Mr. Landers's went down. The waist boat—mine—was left on its davits. But Gabriel, its boatheader, armed with a shoulder gun, went in the mate's boat. Left aboard to help work ship, I had an opportunity to view that exciting chase from beginning to end.

With storm-reefed sails, the boats went plunging away over the big seas, dodging sharply about to avoid the ice cakes. Not more than two hundred yards away on our starboard beam a great whale was blowing. The mate marked it and went for it like a bull dog. He steered to intercept its course. It was a pretty piece of maneuvering. The whale rose almost in front of him and his boat went shooting upon its back. Long John let fly his harpoon. Gabriel fired a bomb from his shoulder gun. There was a flurry of water as the whale plunged under. Back and forth it slapped with its mighty flukes as it disappeared, narrowly missing the boat. Down came the boat's sail. It was bundled up in a jiffy and the mast slewed aft until it stuck out far behind. Out went the sweeps. The mate stood in the stern wielding a long steering oar. I could see the whale line whipping and sizzling out over the bows.

For only a moment the whale remained beneath the surface. Then it breached. Its black head came shooting up from the water like a titanic rocket. Up went the great body into the air until at least forty feet of it was lifted against the sky like some weird, mighty column, its black sides glistening and its belly showing white. Then the giant bulk crashed down again with a smack on the sea that might have been heard for miles and an impact that sent tons of water splashing high in the air. For an instant the monster labored on the water as if mortally hurt, spouting up fountains of clotted blood that splattered over the ice blocks and turned them from snow white to crimson. Then a second time the whale sounded and went speeding away to windward, heading for the ice pack.

It dragged the boat at a dizzy clip despite the fact that the line was running out so fast as to seem to the men in the boat a mere vibrant, indistinct smear of yellow. The boat was taken slicing through the big waves, driving its nose at times beneath the water, and knocking against lumps of ice. A long ice block appeared in its course. A collision seemed inevitable unless the boat was cut loose from the whale. Captain Shorey was watching the chase with fierce intentness as he leaned upon his crutches on the forecastle head. He had been filled with great joy, seized with anxiety or shaken with anger as the hunt passed from one phase to another. He shouted his emotions aloud though there was never a chance for the men in the boats to hear him,

"Good boy, Long John," he had cried when the boatsteerer drove his harpoon home.

"That's our fish," he had chortled as the wounded leviathan leaped high against the sky and spouted blood over the ice.

Now when it seemed possible that the mate would be forced to cut loose from the whale to save his boat from destruction, the captain danced about on his crutches in wild excitement.

"Don't cut that line! Don't cut that line!" he yelled.

Mr. Winchester realized as well as the captain that there was something like $10,000 on the other end of the rope, and he had no idea of cutting loose. Towed by the whale the boat drove toward the ice. The mate worked hard with his steering oar to avoid striking the block. It was impossible. The bow smashed into one end of the ice cake, was lifted out of the water and dragged across to slip back into the sea. A hole was stove in the starboard bow through which the water rushed. The crew thereafter was kept busy bailing.

It was evident from the fountains of blood that the whale was desperately wounded, but its vitality was marvelous and it seemed it might escape. When Mr. Landers saw the mate's line being played out so rapidly he should have hurried to the mate's boat and bent the line from his own tub to the end of the mate's line. As an old whaleman Mr. Landers knew what to do in this crisis, but in such ice and in such high seas he preferred not to take a chance. He was a cautious soul, so he held his boat aloof. The mate waved to him frantically. Long John and Gabriel wigwagged frenzied messages with waving arms.

As for Captain Shorey on his crutches on the forecastle head, when it seemed certain that the whale would run away with all the mate's line and escape, he apparently suffered temporary aberration. He damned old man Landers in every picturesque and fervent term of an old whaleman's vocabulary. He shook his fist at him. He waved a crutch wildly.

"Catch that whale!" he yelled in a voice husky and broken with emotion. "For God's sake, catch that whale!"

All this dynamic pantomime perhaps had its effect on Landers. At any rate, his men began to bend to their sweeps and soon his boat was alongside that of the mate. His line was tied to the free end of the rope in the mate's almost exhausted tub just in time. The mate's line ran out and Landers' boat now became fast to the whale.

Fortune favored Landers. His boat was dragged over the crests of the seas at thrilling speed, but he managed to keep clear of ice. The whale showed no sign of slowing down. In a little while it had carried away all the line in Mr. Landers' tub. The monster was free of the boats at last. It had ceased to come to the surface to blow. It had gone down into the deep waters carrying with it the mate's harpoon and 800 fathoms of manila rope. It seemed probable it had reached the safety of the ice pack and was lost.

The boats came back to the brig; slowly, wounded, limping over the waves. The flying spray had frozen white over the fur clothes of the men, making them look like snow images. They climbed aboard in silence. Mr. Landers had a hang-dog, guilty look. The skipper was a picture of gloom and smoldering fury. He bent a black regard upon Mr. Landers as the latter swung over the rail, but surprised us all by saying not a word.

When the next day dawned, we were out of sight of ice, cruising in a quiet sea. A lookout posted on the forecastle head saw far ahead a cloud of gulls flapping about a dark object floating on the surface. It was the dead whale.

We hope you enjoyed Harry Lauder's *A Minstrel In France*. This edition was entirely redesigned from the text of the original book, published in 1918, although spelling and vernacular were maintained. For additional information and other interesting memoirs from 1500 Books visit our website at www.1500books.net.